CW00531585

TRADEMARKS

TRADEMARKS

Tom Blackett
Deputy Chairman
Interbrand Group Ltd

© Tom Blackett 1998

All rights reserved. No reproduction, copy or transmission of this publication may be made without written permission.

No paragraph of this publication may be reproduced, copied or transmitted save with written permission or in accordance with the provisions of the Copyright, Designs and Patents Act 1988, or under the terms of any licence permitting limited copying issued by the Copyright Licensing Agency, 90 Tottenham Court Road, London W1P 9HE.

Any person who does any unauthorised act in relation to this publication may be liable to criminal prosecution and civil claims for damages.

The author has asserted his right to be identified as the author of this work in accordance with the Copyright, Designs and Patents Act 1988.

First published 1998 by
MACMILLAN PRESS LTD
Houndmills, Basingstoke, Hampshire RG21 6XS
and London
Companies and representatives
throughout the world

ISBN 0–333–72588–3

A catalogue record for this book is available from the British Library.

10 9 8 7 6 5 4 3 2 1
07 06 05 04 03 02 01 00 99 98

Copy-edited and typeset by Povey–Edmondson
Tavistock and Rochdale, England

Printed and bound in Great Britain by
Antony Rowe Ltd
Chippenham, Wiltshire

To Tom and Phyl

'If this business were to be split up, I would be glad to take the brands, trademarks and goodwill and you could have all the cash and bricks and mortar – and I would fare better than you.'

John Stuart
Former Chairman of Quaker

Contents

List of Tables and Figures

Tables

Figures

List of Images

The author and publishers are grateful to the copyright-holders for permission to reproduce the images in the plate section.

Acknowledgements

Sarah Longhorn typed the manuscript for this book with speed and precision and made the numerous alterations required with patience and good humour. John Murphy most kindly reviewed and revised the manuscript with his expert eye and customary rigour. Many colleagues and friends also assisted, notably Janet Fogg, John Peacock and Julie Turner of Markforce Associates, Interbrand's trademark legal consultancy, and Isobel Davies of Eversheds, whose observations on comparative advertising law were invaluable. My colleague Raymond Perrier provided thoughtful notes on brand valuation and internal licensing while Paul Stobart helped with useful tips on preparing brand identity manuals. In addition, many clients gave permission for their names and logos to be shown. Finally my wife B endured many bleak weekends while this 'bending author, with rough and all-unable pen . . . pursued the story'.

TOM BLACKETT

Introduction

In the last two decades of the twentieth century trademarks – or brands as they are familiarly known once they have been used and acquired a 'personality' – have established themselves as by far the most resilient and valuable forms of 'intellectual property'. The rights conferred in trademarks are indefinite – subject to conditions that are far from onerous – and manufacturers, aware of the potency of these rights, have sought to exploit them through brand-building, advertising, promotion and product development in order to create a protectable 'bond' with the consumer. The benefits of such investment have been enormous: customer loyalty, reliable cash flows and steady and growing market share. And as a result, the trademark has become an asset of considerable economic value.

This book is written with the marketing practitioner in mind rather than the specialist lawyer, and in it I have attempted to set down 'best practice' in regard to the development and management of trademarks. However, much emphasis is given to the importance of protecting trademarks from the depredations of third parties – which, if unchecked, can result in serious economic damage to the trademark owner – and to the simple procedures that should be followed in order to reinforce and uphold trademark rights. Considerable emphasis too is given to the creative and strategic aspects of brand development and exploitation, including how the value of a brand can be measured and this information put to good use to the benefit of the brand owner.

I hope, therefore, that this book will provide useful information to all those with an interest in trademarks and brands. These may be students or practitioners of marketing who wish to find out more about the often obscure area of trademark law or, indeed, trademark lawyers interested to learn how valuable their contribution is to the numerous businesses whose fortunes now rest on the success or failure of their brands.

Finally, you will see that throughout this book I have used the single word *trademark*, according to the American convention rather than two separate words *trade mark*, the normal English practice. This contraction has saved a minute part of one tree.

CHAPTER 1

What is a Trademark?

A Definition

A trademark is a name, a sign or a symbol which is used to distinguish the products or services of an enterprise from those of others. A trademark can therefore consist of:

- Words (for example, Coca-Cola, Walkman)
- Letters (for example, AT&T, RTZ)
- Numbers (for example, 4711, No. 5)
- Symbols (for example, The Coca-Cola Dynamic Ribbon device or McDonald's golden arches)
- Signatures (for example, those of Johnnie Walker or Ford)
- Shapes (for example, Toblerone's distinctive triangular-shaped chocolate bar or in the UK, Jif Lemon's squeezy plastic lemon)

A trademark can also consist, in some circumstances, of musical jingles or oral phrases and slogans (such as American Express's 'Don't Leave Home Without It'), colours or combination of colours and even smells. In fact, just about anything can be a trademark as long as it performs the key role of *distinguishing* the products (or services) of one manufacturer from those of others.

In practice, many established products and services are protected not just by a single trademark, for example a distinctive name, but by a series of related trademarks covering, perhaps, the name, its distinctive logostyle and also a slogan or freestanding logo. Coca-Cola is an excellent example: not only is the name a protected trademark, but so too is the distinctive copperplate logostyle (based, it is said, on the signature style of the company's founder, Frank M. Robinson), the 'dynamic ribbon', the highly distinctive waisted bottle, many of the company's slogans (for example, 'It's the real thing') and also its distinctive combination of colours (Images 1–2).

These individual elements in the overall trademark 'mix' can be protected separately, in combination or both. In most instances, however, it is the *name* which lies at the core of a product's trademark protection and which is the single most important element. The reason is that names are, in most instances, much more distinctive than colours, designs, letters, numerals or shapes and much more capable, therefore, of performing the critical distinguishing function.

Getting Maximum Impact

Even though the name itself is in *legal* terms the single most protectable element in most cases, in *marketing* terms the strongest brands are those with a protectable, distinctive name **plus** distinctive design and packaging **plus** strong advertising and communications **plus**, of course, a differentiated and high quality product.

■ Trademarks, Patents, Designs and Copyrights

Trademarks, patents, registered designs and copyrights are all forms of 'intellectual property'. As such they form part of the *intangible* asset base of a company and, with careful nurturing, can acquire value far in excess of such tangible assets as plant, machinery, cash and property. In legal terms, too, intellectual property can be every bit as strong as tangible property; clear and specific legal title can be secured to such assets enabling owners to buy, sell, loan, license and mortgage their intellectual property in much the same way as they might lease out a warehouse or sell off a loss-making subsidiary.

For many companies nowadays, intangible, rather than tangible assets underpin the real 'worth' of the business. A considerable body of law now exists to help companies protect their intellectual property and because such rights frequently lie at the core of brands, an understanding of their legal basis is essential to an understanding of brands. But trademarks are not the same as other types of intellectual property such as patents, registered designs and copyrights and it is necessary to distinguish clearly between these separate but related concepts.

- **Patents** protect inventions. The inventor of a novel and non-obvious idea that is capable of industrial exploitation may be rewarded with a monopoly in the use of that invention, normally for around 20 years.
- **Registered designs** relate to the features of shape, configuration or pattern and ornamentation of a useful article – for example the distinctive shape of a piece of furniture, the pattern or motif on a set of crockery, or the visual appeal of a woven fabric or of a wallpaper. Such designs can normally be protected for up to three consecutive five-year periods.
- **Copyrights** apply to artistic, literary, dramatic and musical works. Normally it is not necessary to register copyright; it exists from the moment the book is written or the score composed. (The exception is the

United States.) However, in order to enforce your rights you have to be able to prove that you do in fact own title and that this has been infringed by a third party. It is therefore essential to retain all the original material such as drawings and drafts in which copyright might reside. Copyright protection generally extends from the time the work is created to 50 years after the death of the author or originator.

- **Trademarks** are words or symbols that are used to distinguish the products or services of one manufacturer or supplier from those of another. By registering a trademark, a supplier can obtain, in that country, a monopoly in his trademark in relation to specified goods and services. Unlike other forms of intellectual property, the period of this monopoly can be unlimited, provided the registration is renewed and otherwise properly maintained.

Brand owners can therefore use a number of different intellectual property rights in order to protect their brands. Eastman Kodak Company, for example, has its brand name protected throughout the world through trademark registration. Certain features of the design of the product or of its packaging will, undoubtedly, be protected by registered designs. The distinctive logo design, as well as being a registered trademark, will also be protected by copyright – as will the technical manuals, original drawings, packaging and advertising materials. And certain of the machines and processes used in the manufacture of Kodak products will be protected by patents. Thus the company can 'ring-fence' its valuable intellectual property and protect it from the depredations of third parties.

Intellectual Property Protection

Patents, registered designs, copyrights and trademarks all provide valuable ways to protect constituent elements of your product, service or brand. Only trademarks, however, have, potentially, an indefinite life and thus can outlive all other forms of intellectual property protection.

■ How the Trademark Fits into the Overall Product 'Mix'

A strong and distinctive trademark – be it a name, sign or symbol, or all three – will in time become inseparable from the product or service it identifies. Thus it becomes as much a part of the product marketing 'mix' as the product itself and acts as a guarantee of quality and authenticity in which buyers can place implicit trust. Companies that fail to recognize this and allow product quality to slip risk destroying the credibility of their trademark and alienating the consumer. It follows, therefore, that in companies with powerful brands and a loyal consumer following, the terms 'product management' and 'brand management' are synonymous.

The role that the trademark plays within the overall product marketing mix is governed by a complex of factors. In many markets, particularly those where a high degree of rationality informs the purchase decision, the role of the trademark has been to encapsulate and represent the origin, quality and authenticity of the product. This perhaps is the traditional role of the trademark – as performed by the potter's mark on an Etruscan vase – that of the 'silent salesperson'. In other markets – particularly modern, well-developed markets for fast moving consumer goods – the trademark has, as we discuss later, an altogether different part to play: that of helping actively to 'add value' to the product or service concerned by creating additional appeals over and above the guarantee of basic needs satisfaction.

Not everyone, however, chooses to promote their trademark with the exuberance of Coca-Cola, the precision of AT&T or the quirkiness of Perrier. Nor should they; it may well be inappropriate and potentially damaging for them to do so. In many cases however a company's culture and beliefs are reflected in the promotion of its trademarks. The Mercedes three-pointed star for example, represents the pursuit of engineering excellence; Legal & General's colourful umbrella symbolizes the traditional insurance market values of watchfulness and protection; IBM's 'big blue' trademark affirms consistency in a changing world, although IBM has now revamped its strategy most successfully, realizing that consistency to the point of inflexibility threatened the future of the company.

Increasingly, the widespread availability of capital and technology makes finding and sustaining a competitive product advantage very difficult. Pharmaceuticals giants like Sandoz, Glaxo Wellcome, Merck and SmithKline Beecham spend billions on research and development in pursuit of the elusive molecule that will provide them with a sustainable advantage over their competitors. Other companies, particularly those with little recourse to patent, design or copyright protection – typically service industries like banking and insurance or 'low technology' industries such as food and drink – are forced to look elsewhere for a sustainable point of difference. It is here where the trademark can be used as a key determinant of choice and as a vehicle for marketing investment.

Thus the trademark has a central role to play in the product mix. Whatever the nuance of this role it remains the prime means of identifying the product or service concerned and, as we have pointed out above, it is the only aspect of a company's intellectual property which is capable of indefinite protection.

Trademarks and the Product 'Mix'

Used as a marketing tool, trademarks are inseparable from the products or services they symbolize; their fortunes are inextricably mixed. The impulse to compete through the aggressive use of trademarks can lift the product out of the 'crowd' and present the company and its products in a new and more dynamic light.

History of Trademarks

Trademarks have existed for almost as long as organized trade. It is said that the Mediterranean and the Middle East was the cradle of civilization and it may well be said that the ancient civilizations of Etruria, Greece and Rome were the cradle of trademarks. Some of the earliest manufactured goods in 'mass' production were clay pots, the remains of which can be found in great abundance in the region. There is considerable evidence among them of the use of trademarks, which in their earliest form were the potter's mark (Image 3), but these gradually became more sophisticated through the use of names or devices from a cross or star. In Ancient Rome, principles of commercial law developed which acknowledged the origin and title of potters' marks but this did not deter manufacturers of inferior quality pots from imitating the marks of well-known manufacturers in order to dupe the public. There are even examples of imitation Roman pottery bearing imitation Roman marks. These pots, which can be seen in the British Museum, were made in Belgium and exported to Britain in the first century AD and were designed to fool the illiterate natives. Thus as trade followed the flag – or eagle – so the insidious practice of unlawful imitation lurked at its heels, a practice which remains commonplace despite the strictures of our modern, highly developed legal systems.

With the collapse of the Roman Empire, the elaborate and highly sophisticated system of trade that had bound together in mutual interdependence the Mediterranean and Northern European countries gradually crumbled. Trademarks and logos continued to be used but mainly on a local scale, the exceptions being the distinguishing marks used by kings and emperors. This was the beginning of heraldry, which first stirred in the Dark Ages, burst into flower in the twelfth century and culminated with the Renaissance. It may seem incongruous to comment on the similarities which lie at the roots of heraldry and trademarks but they are too many to ignore. From heraldry we learn of the desire of an individual or a family to distinguish themselves outwardly by the use of a coat of arms, to show that they had performed some service that exemplified the code of chivalry. From the use of trademarks we learn of the desire of an individual or family to distinguish the goods they own or manufacture by the use of a name or device in order to proclaim their quality and authenticity. The fleur-de-lys in France, the Habsburg eagle in Austria–Hungary (Image 4) and the imperial chrysanthemum in Japan all indicated ownership, patronage and control. At the same time, when the volume production of fine porcelain, furniture and tapestries began in France and Belgium, largely because of royal patronage, trademarks and logos were increasingly used by factories to indicate quality and origin. Heraldic devices and trademarks are thus visual proclamations of origin, ownership, achievement and prestige (Image 6).

However, the widescale use of trademarks and logos is essentially a phenomenon of the late nineteenth and twentieth centuries. The industrial revolution, with its improvements in manufacturing and communications, opened up the civilized world and allowed the mass-marketing of consumer products. Indeed, many of today's best-known consumer brands date from that period. Singer sewing machines, Coca-Cola soft drinks, Bass beer (Image 8), Quaker oats (Image 5), Cook's tours, Sunlight soap, Shredded Wheat breakfast cereal, Kodak film (Image 25), American Express travellers' cheques, Heinz baked beans and Prudential Insurance are just a few examples.

But it is the period since the end of the Second World War, during which profound improvements to the well-being of much of the world's population have occurred, that has seen the real explosion in the use of trademarks and logos. Propelled by the collapse of Communism, the arrival of mass broadcasting systems and greatly improved transport and communications, trademarks and logos have come to symbolize the conversion of most 'Western' economies from command-dominant to demand-dominant, with all the social consequences that this entails. Trademarks and logos, it can be fairly said, have become the ultimate expression of capitalism.

■ Origins of Trademark Law

With the growth in organized trade and the increasing use of trademarks and logos by producers to identify their goods and guarantee their authenticity came the requirement for legal systems to help protect the valuable commercial interests that trademarks represent. The earliest trademarks recognized by statute law in England were hallmarks used by the cutlers of Hallamshire (Sheffield). Regulations regarding the use of such hallmarks were first drawn up during the reign of Elizabeth I and codified by the Cutlers' Company Act of 1623. Under the *common* law, however, remedies for the infringement of unregistered trademarks had been provided for several centuries (the earliest reported case, brought by a clothier, was decided in 1618). But it was not until 1875 that the first British Trade Marks Act was passed. The first trademark registered under the Act was the red triangle for Bass pale ale (Image 8). This famous and enduring symbol features clearly in Manet's painting of the bar at the Folies Bergères (Image 9) and is perhaps an ironic tribute from a country whose own formal trademark legal system dates from as early as 1820.

The 1875 Act has been amended several times. The most notable of these amendments were in 1938, when revisions were adopted which further distanced UK practice from that of its continental neighbours; in 1986, when the provision of statutory protection was extended to owners of *service* marks, thus bringing the UK broadly into line with most other countries; and in 1994 to comply with the EC Trademarks Directive:

The purpose of the EC Trademarks Directive is to harmonize trademark law throughout the European Union and it is hoped that the latest amendment to UK law will:

> '*strengthen protection against counterfeiting, make it simpler and cheaper for businesses to protect their trademarks, ensure that trademarks have the same rights and test for validity everywhere in the single market and introduce simpler procedures at the Patent Office.*' (Department of Trade and Industry)

Trademark law is no different from any other law; it must continue to evolve as the needs of commerce and society change. Since 1938 there has been a huge increase in the sophistication with which trademarks are used by their owners and the way in which they are appreciated by the public. The widescale exploitation of trademarks – by advertising, brand extension, character merchandising and franchising, for example – now means that trademarks have assumed an overall importance in society of which the authors of the 1875 Act could hardly have dreamed.

■ Trademarks, Brand Names, Service Marks

It may at this stage be useful to 'unravel' the terminology that is used when the subject of brands is discussed. Terms like trademark, trade name, service mark, brand, brand name and corporate name are common parlance to legal and marketing people; frequently they are used interchangeably. Yet they do have different meanings, and rather more precision in their use would be widely beneficial. The following glossary may help:

- **A trademark** is a name, a sign or a symbol which is used to distinguish the products or services of an individual or enterprise from those of others.
- **A trade name** is a name which is used to distinguish an individual or enterprise offering goods or services.
- **A service mark** is a trademark used specifically to distinguish a service as opposed to goods.

- **A brand** is a trademark, or combination of trademarks, which through promotion and use has acquired significance over and above its functional role of distinguishing the goods or services concerned.
- **A brand name** is the most common form of trademark and is the central component of the brand.
- **A corporate name** is a company name.

Terms like 'trademark' and 'trade name' tend mainly to be used by those involved in the administration of intellectual property – typically trademark lawyers – while it is marketing people who tend to use the equivalent terms brand name and corporate name.

How the Role of the Trademark Varies by Industrial Sector

The role that trademarks play can differ widely according to the nature of the product or service for which they are used. But whatever the nature of the product or service the trademark must at minimum fulfil its basic task of helping to distinguish the goods (or services) concerned for the benefit of the buyer.

For very many businesses, however – particularly those in highly competitive consumer markets such as foods, drink, fashion and toiletries – the trademark has a much more active role to play in helping to *influence* choice. Such businesses recognize that the values, based on consumers' beliefs, inherent in their brand names can provide them with a potent means of differentiating their products in situations where, often, the products themselves are not too distinguishable. (What *is* the difference between Coke and Pepsi? In terms of taste, the differences are subtle; in terms of brand image, the differences are enormous.)

Thus manufacturers of consumer goods rely heavily upon their trademarks – most commonly their brand names – to provide them with a competitive advantage, and brand names have become a vital part of strategic marketing. Their role has moved on from being a means simply of distinguishing the product or service concerned to a means of adding values that consumers will recognize as uniquely attractive and relevant to their needs. This implies that the brand name can acquire an additional 'emotional' dimension which can influence choice in situations of price and product parity – and the billions of pounds that are spent every year in advertising consumer brands would tend to support this.

In many markets, however, the emotional dimension is not, or cannot be, such an important factor; these are markets where the purchase decision must of necessity be a more informed and rational one, because the element of risk involved in making a wrong choice may be a significant one.

The process involved in acquiring a new car, word processor or fork lift truck are probably very similar. Considerable cost is involved, so careful research must be undertaken and comparisons made between the products available. Clearly the brand does have a role to play in reflecting the reputation of the manufacturer, but ultimately the risk is such that the purchasing decision must be driven by hard facts rather than emotion. (But even here, where near parity exists in terms of price and performance, the brand image can tip the balance at point of sale.)

The consequence of changing your brand of whisky and being disappointed because this proves not to be to your taste, is probably irritation – perhaps rage. Life, however, will go on. The consequence of a doctor prescribing a new drug, without adequate research into its properties and performance, may be far more serious – perhaps life threatening. Again the brand does have a role to play but this is confined to guaranteeing the quality and the origin of the goods; the risk involved makes it incumbent upon the buyer to ensure that the product is right.

The role that brands play can vary widely by industrial sector and can frequently be determined by the degree of risk that attends the purchase decision. The brand can play either a passive role in merely distinguishing the product or service concerned, or an active role in helping to *influence* the purchase decision (Figure 1.1).

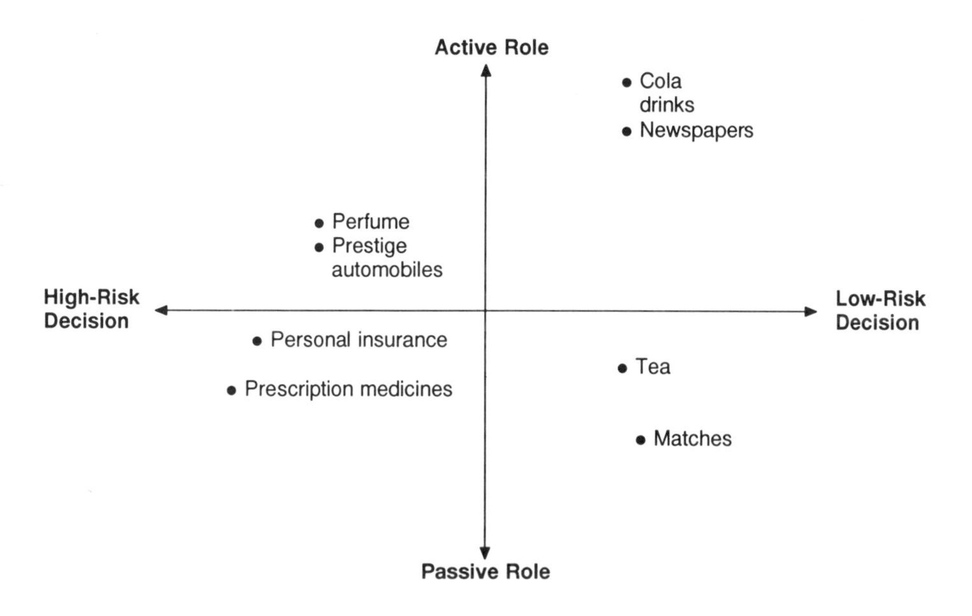

Figure 1.1 The Role of Brands

Irrespective of the level of risk inherent in the purchase decision, the potential for the brand to play an active role in determining choice is always there. This is the challenge for the brand manager.

Word Marks, Initials, Service Marks, and so on

As discussed above, a trademark can consist of a word, letters, numbers, a symbol, a signature, a shape, a slogan or even a musical jingle. In many instances a combination of these may be involved. The adoption, commercial development and exploitation of a trademark can be a long and very expensive business but the rewards can be enormous. It makes good sense therefore to secure for your trademarks the best protection that the law will provide – that is, registration.

A registration is a statutory monopoly in a trademark and to qualify for registration a new trademark must fulfil three important legal requirements; it must be:

- Distinctive.
- Neither descriptive nor misdescriptive of the goods for which it is to be registered and used.
- Different from the existing marks of other traders used or registered for the same or similar goods, so as to avoid confusion or deception.

There is an established hierarchy of trademarks ranging in terms of legal protectability from strong to weak. Four categories are generally recognized, and are, in descending order:

- Invented or arbitrary.
- Suggestive.
- Descriptive.
- Generic.

Invented and arbitrary marks – be they names, designs or shapes – are invariably the strongest types of trademark. The Kodak and Exxon names are pure invention (Images 9 and 25) while the Camel and Green Giant names are not. But the use of Camel in relation to cigarettes and Green Giant in relation to prepared vegetables is arbitrary; neither performs any suggestive or descriptive role whatsoever, their task is simply to indicate the origin of the goods. Similarly the Arm and Hammer device is largely abstract in character, as is the Shell logo; they are inventions, products of the intellect. The law acknowledges the inventiveness of all these trademarks in relation to the goods concerned and confers upon their owners a monopoly in their use. This is what makes invented and arbitrary marks the strongest of all trademarks.

Suggestive marks can combine protectability with the power to communicate. There are numerous famous examples: the Dove soap brand name conjures up impressions of downy softness, and hints subtly that use of the product will benefit the complexion accordingly; the Visa name, used for payment card services and travellers cheques, suggests global accessibility and authenticity; ebullient Monsieur Bibendum of Michelin (Image 10), with his pneumatic rolls of fat, resembles a mountain of compressed motor car tyres; McDonald's 'golden arches device', shaped out of the M in the brand name, is supposed to symbolize a welcome. Suggestive marks represent the middle ground of trademarks, much explored by communications experts seeking to alight upon the name and symbol that will motivate consumers irrespective of culture and nationality, but which are not descriptive and hence unprotectable.

Descriptive marks can certainly communicate, but they tend to be weak legal properties. Names and images which describe the characteristics of the product or service concerned are very popular with marketing and advertising people because they help to 'position' – the first task in communicating a new or existing product. Positioning involves the process of explaining *what* the product or service is, *who* it is for, and *why* it is special and worth the customer's attention. Unfortunately names like Kwik-Fit for a tyre-fitting service (Image 11) or symbols like the globe, used invariably to communicate the wide-ranging nature of the product offer, are not generally given much protection in law. This is because they describe a very general characteristic or attribute of the product (or service) and the law decrees that any trader should have access to and use of such terminology or symbols, freely in the course of his or her business. Descriptive marks do not serve the key trademark function of indicating the source or origin of the product.

The final category is generic marks, to which no one can lay claim. Generic marks comprise simple product descriptions like 'cheese' or 'oil', common dictionary words used to describe 'a class of objects'. They also comprise words which may originally have been trademarks but through neglect or misuse by their owners have lost their uniqueness in relation to the products they once distinguished. Famous examples of former trademarks now in general use as product descriptors are names like klaxon, zip, gramophone and, in some countries, aspirin and thermos. The reason these names have become generics is often because their owners have failed to prevent competitors from using them to describe their own similar products, and thus have undermined their distinctiveness and negated their role of indicating source or origin. We discuss later in this book how to prevent your trademark slipping into generic use.

In addition to descriptive marks and generic marks there are other categories of trademarks which are regarded as legally weak; these are laudatory names, geographical names, common surnames and letters. Again this is because the law will not allow anyone to monopolize – and therefore to deny to others – a name or symbol that is in common use in phonic or visual language and relevant to the product or service concerned. Thus no one is allowed to monopolize the word 'super' in relation to their product; nor can a geographical name – say 'Champagne' in relation to sparkling wine – be registered as a trademark. Likewise a common surname cannot easily be registered as a trademark and it has taken many years of use to qualify the

Smith's brand name for registration. Letters and initials too are considered non-distinctive, although 4711 (Image 12) and IBM, like Smith's, are now registered marks.

In developing a new trademark, therefore, distinctiveness should be the goal. There is very little point in painstakingly and expensively developing a new product or service and then adopting a trademark which your competitors can easily copy. A distinctive trademark can be protected indefinitely, and with it the market position and investment of the trademark owner.

Words, Symbols, Initials, Numbers?

1. Registration allows you to protect the investment you have made in your trademark.

2. Success in registration can greatly be enhanced by selecting a strong trademark that is original for its field.

3. 'Strength' can be calibrated according to the nature of the mark:

   - invented or arbitrary — 80–100 per cent
   - suggestive — 50–100 per cent
   - descriptive — 20–50 per cent
   - generic — 0 per cent

4. Invented, arbitrary and suggestive names and symbols are the strongest forms of trademarks. Numbers, letters, commonplace symbols and descriptive names are the weakest.

CHAPTER 2

How to Create Trademarks

The Role of the Trademark

A trademark has three functions:

- To distinguish the goods or services of the enterprise from those of another.
- To indicate the source or origin of the goods or services.
- To represent the goodwill of the trademark owner and to serve as an indication of the quality of his goods or services.

These functions are best expressed by example. The trademark Palmolive is a well-known brand name for soap in the United Kingdom. The Palmolive mark distinguishes the product from the numerous other soap products on the market; it indicates the source of the product and it represents the quality of the product and the goodwill of the manufacturer. Provided Palmolive soap is of good quality and satisfies the consumer, the chances are that when the time comes to buy again the consumer will choose Palmolive. Brand loyalty will then begin to develop.

Brand loyalty is the Holy Grail for brand managers and advertisers. This is because the market share that arises from brand recognition and appreciation in many cases determines the life or death of a consumer product. Brand owners spend considerable amounts of money on developing a name, promoting it and protecting it, because a strong and attractive brand name can provide an enormous competitive advantage and is therefore a powerful marketing tool. It is also the one element of the marketing 'mix' that never changes. Its power therefore resides in its constancy: advertising campaigns, packaging, promotion – even the product itself – can change over time, but names hardly ever do. Familiarity and consistency are the ingredients that make the world's most successful brands:

> '*Trademarks and brand names are among the few familiar points that consumers have to guide them – they are therefore among the most valuable assets of the manufacturer.*' (Lego Group)

A Trademark Has Three Functions

- To distinguish the product
- To indicate the source or origin of the goods
- To represent the goodwill of the trademark owner

The consistency with which it is used over time can help create an asset of enormous value to its owner.

The Importance of Brand Names

Of all forms of trademark, the brand name is most potent – most potent in terms of its ability to motivate consumers and most potent in terms of the quality of legal protection for which it is eligible. Symbols, too, like the Jolly Green Giant and the Coca-Cola Dynamic Ribbon device, are powerful mnemonics – particularly as they can function on a global basis without the linguistic obstacles that sometimes confront brand names. But the evidence of the last few years suggests that, in the large number of merger and acquisition deals that have taken place involving branded goods companies, it has been the brand names which have attracted the substantial premiums paid.

It should be considered too that in planning the development of new products and services, the brand name is the one element of the 'marketing mix' that cannot be changed; there is no margin for error. This is in contrast to other elements of the mix – the product, price, packaging, advertising, even the management team! All these can be modified to sharpen the competitiveness of the new product after its introduction to the market – and they frequently are. But to change the brand name would involve withdrawing the product from the market place, with all that this would entail in terms of wasted investment, loss of prestige and damage to morale.

The Importance of Brand Names

- The name is the one element of the 'marketing mix' that cannot be changed without considerable cost.
- Great care is therefore needed in ensuring that, for new products and services, the brand name is capable of fulfilling the complex strategic and legal role it must play.

It is clear, therefore, that in view of the pivotal role that the brand name plays, great care must be taken to ensure that nothing in the course of developing the new name is left to chance. A proper process is required which takes into account the complex marketing and legal role the name must play.

Different Types of Brand Name

As discussed earlier, brand names can vary widely in their ability to communicate messages about the product or service concerned (see Figure 2.1). The brand name Kodak is a pure invention. It is a collection of letters which is strong, both phonetically and visually, distinctive and memorable, yet is meaningless:

> *'I knew a trade name must be short, vigorous, incapable of being misspelled to an extent that will destroy its identity and, in order to satisfy trademark laws, it must mean nothing. The letter K had been a favorite with me – it seemed a strong, incisive sort of letter. Therefore, the word I wanted had to start with K. Then it became a question of trying out a great number of combinations of letters that made words starting and ending with K. The word Kodak is the result.'* (George Eastman)*

Whatever its provenance Kodak is a classic 'coined' name, capable of excellent trademark legal protection.

The name Sunsilk is by no means a pure invention. It draws its strength from images of softness and associations with the great outdoors. Sunsilk is a classic suggestive name and it too is capable of trademark protection.

Sweet 'n' Low, however, is almost a purely descriptive name. Because it alludes directly to generic attributes of the product (a low-calorie sweetener) it is not eligible for strong legal protection.

In developing brand names for new products companies are frequently drawn to those sorts of names which will help them quickly and easily to communicate the features and benefits of the new product or service and thus 'position' it within its market. They seek names therefore which describe product attributes, preferably in an attractive way. But the weakness of this sort of name is that it is difficult, if not impossible, to protect in law and it lays the way open to imitations.

---

* Interestingly, the Kodak company suggest that the more likely explanation for Eastman's fondness for the letter K is that his mother's maiden name was Kilbourn. It is known that he was particularly grateful to his mother for bringing him up single-handed in difficult circumstances after the premature death of his father.

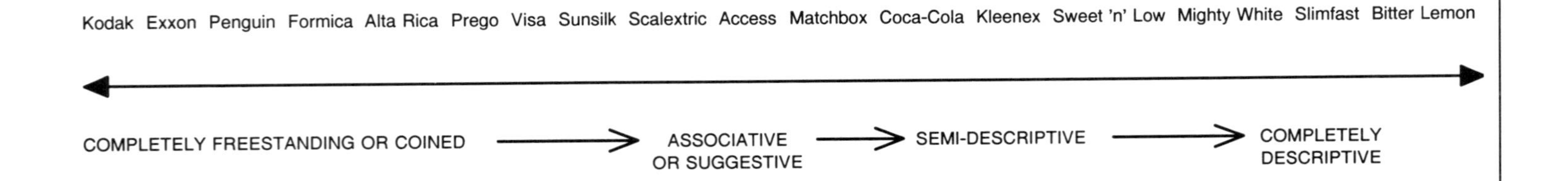

Figure 2.1 The Brand Name Spectrum

Completely freestanding, arbitrary or coined names (like Kodak) can enjoy extremely good legal protection. Yet they are costly to explain and it can frequently take many years of advertising and exposure before the name becomes recognized as synonymous with the product – risking, in the meantime, the chance that consumers may adopt their own, more user-friendly, terminology for the product. The strength of these names – their legal robustness and their ability frequently to assume 'quasi-generic' status (like Hoover) – is also their weakness; and it is a brave marketing executive nowadays who would argue for the advertising budget required to bring such names to life.

The middle route, the associative (or suggestive) route can and does result in powerful, attractive and protectable brand names. Mr Eastman's invention was a novel one – but it is likely that he would have been just as successful with an associative name like Vista. Would he, however, have fared so well with Super-Pic or Easy-Foto, both names which his many subsequent competitors would have found easy to imitate?

The Psychology of Names

How is it that some names have the ability to reach into the psyche and trigger an emotional response that far exceeds mere recognition of the product or service they are used to identify? Why is it that names as disparate in character as Kalashnikov, Badedas and Rolls-Royce are so much more evocative than Thompson, Radox and Ford? Is it merely because, through familiarity, we have come to recognize that such names symbolize products with very special qualities – or is it because of something in the names themselves? This is the psychology of names.

Shakespeare gave Juliet the famous line 'that which we call a rose, by any other name would smell as sweet' (and an unknown Hollywood scriptwriter gave Groucho Marx the line 'a hamburger by any other name would cost twice as much'). The fact that Romeo is a Montague means that, for all his graces, he is unacceptable to Juliet's Capulet family. Juliet resented bitterly the sheer arbitrariness of names and their power to determine fate.

In terms of human psychology we can easily recognize that our names are more than just the labels our parents attach to us. We *live* our names, we *are* our names. Think of the upset we cause when we call someone by the wrong name. In his biography of Sigmund Freud, Ernest Jones writes about himself: 'when a patient addresses me as Dr Smith, I know exactly what he thinks about me'. Think how, over time, a mass of images and associations accumulate round a name. John F. Kennedy, for example, or Oscar Fingal O'Flahertie Wills Wilde, conjure up whole eras as well as the personalities themselves, while other names seem to be little more than a single vivid image: Pontius Pilate, or Sodom and Gomorrah.

Names become intrinsic; names become identity. There is a story told about Captain Cook discovering some Pacific Islanders who had no knowledge of how to navigate by the stars. He taught them and, being practical people, they learned quickly; but the most difficult and puzzling thing for them was understanding how, in the first place, Cook had found out the names of the stars.

As for culture and fashion, think of children's names. Many girls are now named after flowers – Daisy, Violet, Rose – as they were at the beginning of this century, but few children are given the wartime favourites, Jean, Sheila and Norma. What of the aggressive names of the punk era – the Sex Pistols, The Damned, The Stranglers? If you launched a pop group today, would you seriously consider calling them 'Debauchery' or 'Vomit'? Can you imagine that Tommy Dorsey would have hired a singer called Prince or Sting? And, although they were born out of necessity, we now have a current fashion for exotic names – Ysatis, Xeryus, Xantia – which sound as if they come from the Rubaiyat of Omar Khayyam or Coleridge's Kubla Khan.

Many manufacturers, producers and providers of services nowadays recognize the power of names and how the right name can provide a competitive advantage. They base their choice of name for their new product not just on its ability to communicate – for example, Supersaver – but on its ability to motivate – for example, Liquid Gold. The latter, with its overtones of gold – perhaps black as well as gold ingots – is redolent of smooth and effortless success, the absence of risk and easy access. It is the answer to a saver's prayer. Similarly Kalashnikov summons up the rattle and clatter of a light machine gun, Badedas hints at the all-encompassing embrace of the bath, and Rolls-Royce conjures up smoothness and style. All of these names excel through their phonetic construction or the parallel associations they evoke.

Such names of course succeed because there already exists within the language and culture of the listener sets of sounds and images which help build expectations and beliefs. These expectations and beliefs are shaped by experience which in itself is the product of knowledge and receptiveness. The explanation therefore is almost wholly rational – pleasant sounds and images will create agreeable expectations; if these are matched in an appropriate way then a symbiotic relationship may result to the lasting benefit of the brand owner (a fact that has not been lost on such successful manufacturers as Schweppes).

Psychologists such as Sapir and Newmann have suggested that it is the componentary – rather than the construction – of words that can carry 'phonetic symbolism'. Put simply this means that certain vowels and consonants 'sound bigger' than other and so create a particular expectation. Sapir took pairs of meaningless word forms, such as 'mal' and 'mil', which are identical except for the vowel sound. He told his subjects – the people he persuaded to act as guinea pigs in his experiment – that *mal* and *mil* meant table (in an unspecified language). The subjects were asked to indicate which of the words meant 'large table' and which meant 'small table'. The result of the experiment was that 80 per cent of the time the words with the 'a' sound (he used the long 'ah') were found to indicate the larger object, and with the 'i' sound smaller object. He concluded that these sounds have a feeling-significance and a certain meaning in themselves.

Newmann enlarged upon Sapir's work and used more sophisticated statistical methods. As well as confirming from the data he collected that the symbolic value ascribed to different sounds is 'mechanical', depending on resonance and articulation, he showed that phonetic symbolism may be a feature of some languages and not of others. From his parallel exercises in French and in English we may conclude that the content of the English language, being more eclectically formed, is more embracing of phonetic symbolism than that of the French language.

Overall, names are made of single syllables, or connected syllables. These syllables are never neutral, never devoid of meaning or value. Indeed any given name may represent a wealth of meanings, whether merely referential, symbolic, associative, or combinations of these. That is part of the seemingly infinite resource of language.

The Psychology of Names

Descriptive names like Kall Kwik or Kleeneze flit lightly over the surface of life; they fail meaningfully to intrude. Names like Kalashnikov or Kodak however, because of their subtle onomatopoeia or sheer originality, embed themselves in our consciousness and acquire much deeper symbolic value.

■ National/International Aspects

The increasing concentration of world trade into 'blocs' – be these political (for example, the European Union) or geographical – greatly enhanced production and distribution systems, media overlaps and growing convergence in consumer tastes and expectations, means that no marketing executive can ignore the opportunities that are now available for international brands.

Brands that are known to be international in scope exert very particular appeals with consumers. It is probably true that most international brands perform better than their local equivalents, but there is also another closely related factor, less rational but no less compelling. Somehow the knowledge that consumers elsewhere, often in dramatically different economic and cultural circumstances, enjoy the same satisfactions that we derive from a Mars Bar, say, or a Hertz rental car, is at once comforting and beguiling. International brands – almost irrespective of category – have a cachet with which local brands find it most difficult to compete.

This is the power of international brands; and the value they bring their owners is reflected in better returns on investment and in the firm base they provide for future business development (Table 2.1 and Image 15).

So, in planning new brands, the consideration that your interesting new product or service could at some stage enter wider international markets should be borne closely in mind when developing the new brand's name. This has implications regarding the linguistic and legal criteria that are set for the new name, and these are discussed in the next chapter.

Attractions of International Brands

- Scale economies.
- Improved distribution.
- Media overlaps and satellite broadcasting.
- Converging tastes and expectations.

International brands have very special appeals – and the opportunity for international brands has never been better. But these must be carefully planned.

Table 2.1 The World's Most Valuable Brands are International

		1996 Value (US$ bn)
1.	Marlboro	44.6
2.	Coca-Cola	43.4
3.	McDonald's	18.9
4.	IBM	18.5
5.	Disney	15.4
6.	Kodak	13.3
7.	Kellogg's	11.4
8.	Budweiser	11.0
9.	Nescafé	10.5
9.=	Intel	10.5

Source: Financial World/Interbrand.

Criteria for a Strong Brand Name

The criteria are as follows. A strong brand name must be:

- **Distinctive** – it should distinguish the product or service concerned.
- **Appropriate** – it should support the market positioning of the new product or service – or at least should not conflict with this.
- **Appealing** – it should help to stimulate interest in the new product or service and motivate trial.
- **Linguistically acceptable** – it should be free from inappropriate meanings in all the countries where it will be used.
- **Legally protectable** – it should be available to use, register and protect in all countries of interest.

These are all vital – if general – requirements. In addition to these the brand name has a very specific strategic role to play. This is to help position the new product or service in a way that underlines its competitive points of difference.

Thus the role of the brand name is essentially complex; it must satisfactorily perform a number of quite different functions. Drawing these elements together can only successfully be achieved by adopting an integrated, strategic approach to developing the brand name.

Creating Strong Brand Names

- Brand names are a complex of different, sometimes conflicting, elements.
- Successful name creation is not a random process (leave that to astrophysics!).
- An integrated, strategic approach is required that acknowledges the strategic, linguistic and legal imperatives involved.

Developing a Brand Name Strategy

The dictionary defines *strategy* as 'generating, or the art of conducting, a campaign or gaining an advantage'. In this instance the advantage we seek is a superior brand name which contains all the elements referred to in the previous section. As these elements are disparate it is clear that the quality of 'generalship' displayed must be of a high order – but at the same time sensitive to the complexity of the task.

How then do you develop a brand name strategy? The first stage is information gathering and this should cover:

- **The product or service** What is the new product concept and what is special about it? To whom will it appeal and why? Who are the competitors and on what basis is the new product superior? Through which outlets will it be sold and through which media will it be communicated? What is the desired 'personality' (tone of voice) of the new brand?
- **Market** How is the market constructed – is it fragmented or concentrated? Is the market new or long-established? What is the overall trend in the market and is the market stable or volatile? What is the current and potential geographical scope of the market?
- **Countries of interest** In which countries is trademark registration to be sought? In which cultures and languages must the name be particularly appropriate? What is the message or messages to be communicated by the name? Which messages can be communicated by other means (for example, advertising, packaging, logos, symbols, and so on)? What are the existing competitive trademarks? What constraints are there on the length of the new name and are any particular phonetic or graphic qualities sought?

Once these issues relating to the strategic (that is, marketing) and technical (that is, legal) aspects of the new name have been considered, clearly identified objectives for the naming of the product or service under consideration should be set out and agreed. Next the process of achieving these, within the constraints of the strategy, can commence.

Get a Strategy!

- Governments, armies, businesses and so on operate strategically in order to succeed.
- The process of naming a new product is no different.
- Successful brand naming depends upon careful planning.
- Planning involves two steps:
  – understanding the task and
  – defining the objectives.
- The next stage involves making use of resources.

Developing Creative Themes

Once the brand name strategy has been agreed, initial creative work can commence. This involves the development of a naming brief which, in addition to a description of the product or service to be named and its market positioning, will contain ideas for creative themes which might usefully be explored. In the case of a new shampoo, for example, a range of options may be considered covering 'fresh and natural', 'clinical effectiveness', 'luxuriance', or downright 'sex appeal'. Each one of these themes is rich in evocation and therefore each can be divided according to those naming routes which might prove most fruitful.

In order to choose between these alternative and quite different branding themes, it is important to decide precisely what 'personality' is sought for the new product. This is because the brand name is central to a product's personality and thus has to work with other means of communication, such as media, advertising and packaging, to produce a consistent and enduringly attractive image that will continue to please consumers over the years.

Care must therefore be taken to avoid names which, while attractive and contemporary at the time of their selection, fail to stand the test of time. For example, it might be unduly restrictive to the development of the brand's personality if a name was chosen to express overt 'green' values. Times and issues change, and to choose such a name might risk isolating the brand in a marketing 'timewarp' from which no amount of advertising or design creativity could rescue it. A name like 'Body Shop', however, while reflecting green values, is sufficiently benefit-specific to allow subtle repositioning in line with prevailing attitudes and preferences without undermining the basic retail concept.

Potential creative themes may well already have emerged from previous qualitative research which can in turn enhance these themes. Certainly in our experience, a variety of quite different creative routes can be followed, each of which has its own varied implications in positioning and differentiating the product. Much of the skill involved in selecting the right brand name lies in researching and exploring the widest possible array of routes – many of which may not at first appear to be obvious. Indeed many of the world's strongest brand names are very far from 'obvious'. Who on earth would have selected the Apple name by pursuing a narrow, logical approach?

The brand name is central to the new product's personality and is the one element of the brand which can never change. Choosing the right brand name is therefore critical to the success of the new product – and selecting the right creative theme is key to developing the right brand name.

■ Creative Techniques

Specialist brand name development companies are increasingly being used to develop both national and international brand names. Such consultants will normally start by examining in detail the company's plans for the new product or service, and its marketing objectives and trademark policies; they will then prepare and agree a naming strategy. Once the brand name development task is clearly defined, work starts on creating new names.

Building Creative Themes

The product	Extra strength lager			
The consumer	Male	✓	Female	✗
Points of difference	High ABV	✓	Flavour	✓
Creative themes	Potency		Richness	
	Fast cars		Subtlety	
	Birds of prey		Mouth feel	
	Controlled aggression		Sensuality	
	The 'ultimate'		The 'odd one'	
	and so on		and so on	

Build creative themes on points of difference; try to express these imaginatively in a subtle but accessible way; look for convergences, such as potency and sensuality (above); these can produce names with real depth.

■ Brainstorming

The most productive starting point for the creative process, and a useful method for exploring existing themes and searching for possible new ones, is the use of carefully selected and managed creative, or focus, groups. For international projects focus groups would be organized on an international basis and each group would be led by a trained psychologist skilled in this area. All members of a particular group are usually of one nationality and are specially chosen for their skills with language. Their task is to develop words, word roots, analogies, phrases and ideas in line with the chosen creative themes. In the course of a creation session lasting two or three hours, a group of six to eight people will create a great mass of verbal raw material – perhaps 500 names in total. Eight or ten such groups may be held and the material produced by the groups would be carefully examined for themes, words, concepts, word roots and associations of significance in the different languages.

■ Copywriting

Taking those 'raw' ideas that seem to work best in relation to the agreed strategy copywriters would then start work. Their task would be to develop names which embody the central idea of each creative theme and are thus capable of helping to position the new product in the desired fashion. Literacy, a knowledge of languages – particularly Latin, which underpins most Western languages – verbal dexterity and the capacity for lateral thought are all important requirements for a good copywriter. These skills, supported by a library of relevant source material – technical manuals, foreign language and synonym dictionaries, thesauri, atlases, studies of ancient civilizations, and so on – can, when properly harnessed, produce ideas of startling originality for even the most 'unexciting' of products. Mazurka for a software program, Potenza for a diesel engine and Dialogue, for an anti-depressant drug, are all examples of names which have sprung from this process. Each of these names, because of the appropriate and recognizable meaning that lies at their roots, is ideal for investment with brand imagery – a powerful differentiating factor.

Another good example is Hob-Nobs. Up to a few years ago the culture of branding in the UK biscuit market was essentially descriptive: products were identified by use of a generic title, such as 'digestive', and differentiated only through use of the manufacturer's name and pack design (although even the pack designs in use a few years ago were very similar). Then McVitie's introduced Hob-Nobs, and the whole culture of branding was dramatically changed. By adopting a name which sought to communicate fun and enjoyment, rather than merely describe the product, McVitie's, with Hob-Nobs, became the first volume biscuit manufacturer to create a true brand personality for its new product, an original and highly successful strategy that provided genuine differentiation and consumer appeal.

■ Computer Name Generation

Even though name creation groups can provide clear evidence that the current culture of branding in any particular sector is inappropriate or unexciting, and fresh creation work can be organized to move along newly defined naming themes, we have found that computer techniques can be used productively in three specific areas:

- To search existing data bases and computerized dictionaries.
- To identify names which possess the required attributes (for example, masculine, international, stylish, exotic, and so on).
- To take existing names and use phonetically-based, word-splicing techniques to build new and more interesting names from existing 'core' names.

Many organizations have experimented in the past with computer name generation techniques. It is tempting for firms like Procter & Gamble or Bristol-Myers to believe that somehow by using a computer to generate names they can effectively reserve for themselves all the good names in any particular sector. In practice, computer name generation programs in the past have tended simply to take vowel/consonant constructions plus some popular letter strings and run all the permutations. Millions of names can be generated in this way but most are totally useless. One major company ran what it thought was a simple program to find a name for a new soft drink. So many names were developed that they estimated one person reading at normal speed for eight hours a day would need four months to go through the output just once!

Mechanistic computer name creation programs are of some limited value in naming pharmaceuticals or chemicals. Most brand names, however, need to have a qualitative element, to be associated in some way with the product or its performance or the satisfactions the product brings. To be useful, therefore, computers need to work within such qualitative parameters and thus need to rely on a database of names coded with reference to the qualities of those names. Computer name generation, too, needs to take account of natural language, phonetics and linguistics. Access to computerized synonym and foreign language dictionaries can also greatly enhance the quality of output and assist with name creation.

Creative Techniques

There are three main techniques:

- Brainstorming.
- Copywriting.
- Computer name generation.

But all sources are valid – from the chairman's wife to the postboy – and the wider you search within the scope of your naming strategy, the greater your chances of success.

Selecting a Shortlist

Stage one in developing a new brand name, therefore, is to decide what job you want the new name to perform, now and in the future. Stage two is to isolate those naming themes relevant to the consumer and appropriate in branding and positioning terms. Stage three is to use focus groups, copywriters, computers and an existing name library to create names. Since one focus group alone can develop 500 or more potential names and a short computer run can produce many thousands more, how does one cope with the super-productivity of the creation process?

Brand name development necessarily involves a careful refining process – a great deal of ore has to be fed into the hopper in order to produce a small amount of pure gold – the attractive, strong, protectable brand name. Thus having created a vast list of names it has to be pared down to manageable proportions. To do this, those words are eliminated which at first sight have inherent defects of pronunciation, legibility, memorability or meaning. We would also eliminate all those words that are unregistrable as trademarks, which are too close to existing competitive marks or which fail to meet other broad criteria, such as length.

The next stage would be to present to our client 20 to 30 names which reflect the creative themes pursued and invite his comments. Then, based on those names and themes which were felt to be closest to meeting the agreed strategy, the naming brief would be amended and further creative work carried out.

The final stage of the name creation process would be to select and present a list of 20 to 25 'recommended' names, this time tightly screened against very specific criteria – particularly their acceptability in the major European languages and the absence of any identical and semi-identical trademark registrations in the specific 'classes' of interest.

These names would be discussed and a shortlist of around 15 names agreed for further language checks, full legal searches and consumer testing.

Selecting a Shortlist

- Remember that the 'Eureka Syndrome' does not exist in name selection.
- Just because a name hits you between the eyes does not mean that that it will be linguistically acceptable and legally available for you to use – Murphy's Law almost certainly means that it will not!
- Select 15–20 names for in-depth language checks, full legal searches and consumer testing. If the creation process has been conducted in a focused and imaginative way, any of these 'candidates', subject to the checks, will be capable of doing the job in hand.

Language Checks

Many of us have heard rumours of such wonderful products as Zit (a Cypriot soft drink), Kräpp (Swedish lavatory paper), Nora Knackers (Norwegian crispbread), Super Piss (a Finnish product for unfreezing car locks – although it is rumoured that the real thing is equally effective) and Bum (Spanish potato crisps). Indeed, encountering such exotic brands is one of the more obscure pleasures of international travel. It may be a little unfair to criticize these brands when the owners probably had no intention of marketing them outside their home markets and are not concerned that their brands occasion mirth among visiting foreigners (Images 16–19). However, the world is shrinking fast and no one nowadays – irrespective of whether they intend to confine distribution of their new product to the home market or to open it up on an international scale – can afford to ignore the necessity for careful linguistic testing.

Nor should this be done by recourse to the nearest French, German or Italian dictionary – such sources rarely reveal the secondary and tertiary meanings of words or if the word has a vernacular meaning which may be transitory within the language. Accordingly, it is imperative to check the names with three or four residents of each country concerned, who preferably are representative of the new product's target market.

The need to do this with great care and attention to detail was brought home to us a few years ago. We had developed a shortlist of names for a new high performance motorcycle tyre which would be marketed primarily in Europe. All the names tested well until we interviewed a small group of Dutch 'bikers'. To them one of the names on the list was clearly a non-starter because, among their small but influential group, it was a slang term for an exceptionally delicate part of the female anatomy!

Language Checks

Check names for:

- Pronounceability.
- Meaning.
- Suitability.

in the languages of all countries of interest – and at least in the main European languages and 'American English'. You may not intend your new brand to travel – but who knows what opportunities the future may bring?

Trademark Searching

The next stage should be to take the names which have passed unscathed through the language tests and commence detailed legal availability searches in the registers of the countries of interest.

The availability of a name depends upon whether the identical or a confusingly similar name has already been registered or, in some jurisdictions (notably the USA, UK and other common law-based countries) used by another party on the same or similar products. It is therefore necessary, before adopting a name, to conduct thorough searches to determine what marks have already been registered or used in the markets of interest in relation to similar goods and which might give rise to problems.

Your trademark legal adviser can conduct these searches and any subsequent investigations which may be necessary. If carried out on an international basis, such searches can be both expensive and time-consuming. They should not, however, be avoided – to do so would be to jeopardize the whole project.

To determine whether a mark is available in the USA, for example, counsel will conduct a search of the records of the Patent and Trade Mark Office, trade directories, state trademark registers, 'phone books and other similar sources. A professional search firm with an established library containing such information will almost always be engaged by counsel to conduct the search. The final determination as to whether the mark is available, however, is a legal conclusion which should be made only by experienced trademark counsel.

In reviewing a search report and prior to rendering an opinion on availability, counsel will look at a number of factors:

- The nature of the goods or services in question.
- Their relationship to the goods or services covered by any potentially conflicting mark.
- The similarity of the marks in sight, sound or meaning.
- The exclusivity of the cited mark.
- The inherent strength of the cited mark.
- Whether a potentially confusing mark cited in the search report is, in fact, in use.
- Any history of prior litigation concerning the proposed mark.

As a rule of thumb, if the goods are identical and the marks are identical or very similar, counsel will in all probability reject the proposed mark. On the other hand, where the goods are completely unrelated and the marks are distinguishable, counsel will generally approve the mark. Where the goods appear unrelated, but the marks are similar, counsel must determine whether the co-existence of the proposed mark and the prior mark could result in confusion as to the source of origin of the goods. Additionally, counsel must also consider whether the mark itself is weak or strong. A strong mark would be entitled to more deference than a weak one. Distinctive marks like Xerox, Kodak and Exxon, for example, enjoy a much wider 'zone of protection' than suggestive or descriptive marks such as Teltronic, Supa-Sava or Compu-Max.

The fact that a name of interest is already registered by another party does not necessarily mean that the name is unavailable. It simply means that another party at some stage has registered an interest in the name for particular goods or services. The interest may have waned and the registration may no longer be effective, or the company may have gone out of business or into another kind of business. In such cases it may be relatively easy to acquire the earlier trademark and with it the statutory and other rights of the earlier proprietor.

Negotiations with the owner of an already registered conflicting mark, or action to remove that mark from the register in order to clear the proposed usage, can often take many months to resolve. Important time can therefore be wasted if, at the end of the negotiations, the potential conflict is not resolved. It can also sometimes be costly to clear a name for usage by acquiring the rights established by the owners of existing marks. Generally speaking, if the proposed mark is already registered, it may be best simply to abandon it.

Trademark Searching

Trademark searching is

- An indispensable part of the brand name development process.
- The cost and complexity of a multi-country search programme can be high.
- It is sensible therefore to undertake the searches on a sequential basis: all the names would be searched in the first country, the survivors only in the next country, and so on.
- Careful planning and analysis is required – trademark searching is a job best left to experts!

■ Consumer Testing

A final procedure normally followed before a brand name is selected is detailed testing. Testing potential brand names for products or services which do not currently exist is exceptionally difficult and there is a real danger that consumers will attribute the highest scores in a research situation to familiar-sounding brand names and reject those that are more innovative. (It has been argued that if Steve Jobs had used conventional brand name testing techniques Apple Computer would have been called IRG Corporation or Compumax or some similarly unexciting name; and that if Dior had researched Poison consumers would have rejected this bold name in favour of a name like Passion or L'Amour). Remember the old *Punch* cartoon which had two British 'labouring types' (as they were called in that less politically correct era) glaring suspiciously at a sumptuously attired French visitor. ''Ere Bill, it's a foreigner' Albert cries. ''Eave 'alf a brick at 'im!'. We still react in this way to the unfamiliar.

So name research tends to favour the descriptive and the familiar. Distinctive names are often rejected due to strangeness and original names often lack relevance to the product category in the consumers' minds. Analysis is therefore very important. There are many techniques employed. At Interbrand, we have developed a proprietary technique called Nometrics™, which was devised on the basis of many years' experience of creating and testing names. The technique can be applied both qualitatively or quantitatively.

The most important test criteria in the Nometrics™ name evaluation approach are:

- Pronounceability.
- Scriptability (or particular relevance to the ethical pharmaceutical industry).
- Imagery conjured up.
- Negative associations.
- Likely service/product areas suggested.
- Similarity to existing names.
- Fit to brand concept.
- Memorability.

The analysis of all the above criteria in the light of objectives agreed at the start of the exercise should mean that the research can be used to help with the selection of a name. However, research must not dictate the answer, as the solutions are often not black and white; there can often be other influencing factors which have a role to play in the final selection, such as: legal problems, fit within current company brand hierarchy, other future launches and extensions and the future that the company envisages for the brand.

Wherever possible, a carefully simulated marketing mix test should be carried out prior to choosing the final brand name. In these tests it is important to remember that consumers buy brands, not products, and that a brand is a successful blend of a variety of appeals: the product itself, the brand name, the packaging, the price and the promotion. To test brand names successfully they must, therefore, be placed in the context of the overall brand and not examined in isolation. Consumers, in order to understand and evaluate a proposed brand name, need to understand the rationale for the brand and how the brand will be used in the marketplace. Thus proper stimulus materials are required, such as comprehensive three-dimensional packs, together with proposition boards or animatics that look like real advertisements. The new product concept and the new brand name need to be portrayed as clearly and realiztically as possible. The more help you are able to give consumers in understanding your brand, the better placed they will be to provide you with an informed assessment of your brand name ideas.

However, it is not just how you present your brand name ideas to consumers which is important, it is also how you interpret the results. Consumers have great difficulty in spontaneously fitting new name ideas within their existing

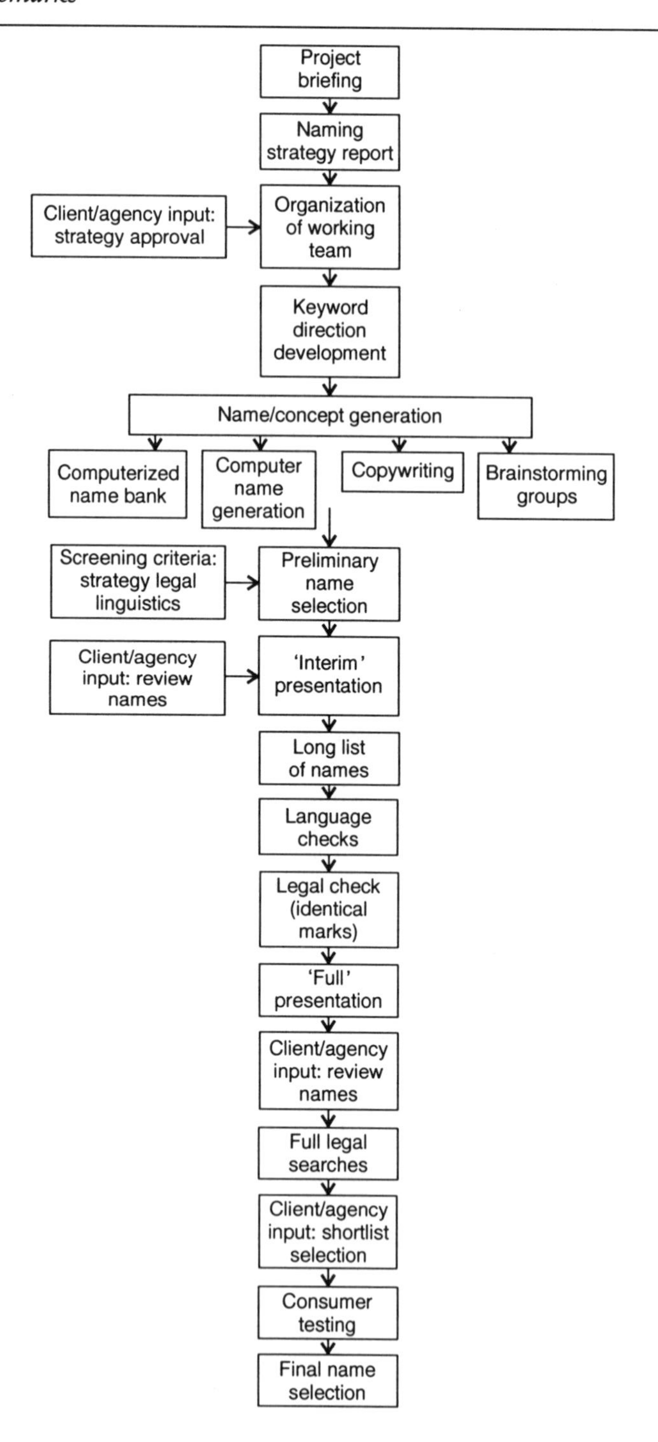

Figure 2.2 The Name Development Process

frame of reference and they tend therefore to prefer the familiar – even the banal – and to reject more innovative names. They prefer too to favour descriptive names as these are more readily understood. They also like to criticize and to show how smart they are by offering spurious objections: 'Snickers sounds like underwear – what's that got to do with a chewy toffee and nuts bar?'; 'I don't see what virginity has got to do with airlines!'. Objections of this sort should normally not be taken at their face value.

At the end of the day, developing new brands is essentially a creative process, with a strong legal component. Good research can certainly help, but only up to a point. Good branding is often about thinking ahead of the consumer, shaping his or her needs and desires and presenting propositions to the consumer which, with familiarity and exposure, become attractive and desirable. In the final analysis, the marketing professional must exercise his or her own judgement based on familiarity with the market, intuition, input from the consumer, assistance from trademark professionals and a real determination to create a well-differentiated brand property.

Consumer Testing

- Developing new brands is essentially a creative process – good research can help but only up to a point.
- Understand therefore the limitations of research. Consumers are essentially conservative and have to understand the rationale for the brand name, or the likelihood is that they will reject it as 'unfamiliar'.
- Remember that consumers buy brands – not products – and that brands are a mix of attributes.
- Test brand names within the context of the overall brand – product, packaging, price, promotion – and not in isolation.

Developing Brand Names for New Drugs

While the name development, checking and testing 'process' described above can be applied to any form of product, service or business, it is worth considering the special needs of the pharmaceutical industry.

In recent years one of the most significant changes in the industry has been the growing use of branding techniques to build awareness of and interest in a new drug. These techniques are designed not only to establish a product in a competitive therapy area (for example, Valtrex in the highly competitive antiviral market) but also to help protect the drug post-patent. One of the most noticeable features of this interest in branding is the use of strong brand names on new drug products.

In the past, brand names generally reflected the generic compound, but today trademarks are becoming much more innovative. Two brand names which stand out as excellent examples of this process, and which happen to be in competition with each other, are the anti-emetic product sold by SmithKline Beecham, branded Kytril but with the generic name of granisetron, and the anti-emetic sold by Glaxo with the brand name Zofran and the generic name ondansetron. Neither of these brand names bears any resemblance to the generic name and this is good. This innovative approach allows both brand names to be more easily protected by law, and also discourages generic intrusion through substitution. In addition, the names are very creative and different, yet are not difficult to pronounce, write or spell – very important criteria for a good drug trademark. Since physicians will have to write and pronounce the brand name many times in their daily routine, a company must make the trademark as easy to remember as it is to spell and pronounce. These are three very important priorities in developing brand names which will help to make them successful.

Another trademark philosophy, which has surfaced with the advent of generics, has been the development of brand names indicative of what disease the product is useful in treating. For example, in recent years, a product has been developed for use in the treatment of asthma, which was branded Serevent – 'Sere' suggesting 'serenity' and 'Vent' indicating that the drug should be used for patients with breathing difficulties. Another example of a brand name indicating the use of a drug is Imigran, for the treatment of migraine. These are two powerful examples of pre-emptive pharmaceutical branding – differentiated, international, and a 'tough act' for other pharmaceutical and generic companies to follow.

■ International Brands

There are several methods of establishing a strong trademark franchise in the pharmaceutical industry. A relatively new philosophy is to try to establish an identical trademark all over the world. One must emphasize the word 'try' because companies are not always successful in registering the same trademark for a specific product all over the world. Many of the major pharmaceutical companies operate in 50 or more countries around the world. This presents a problem in that what may seem to be a good name for a product in English may be a totally unacceptable name in another language. Sometimes only a letter or two will have to be changed in one or two languages to solve the problem and, in effect, the brand name will be seen as a worldwide trademark. However, this is not always the case. When the exact trademark cannot be used in three or more of the major pharmaceutical markets of the world (the USA, UK, Italy, France, Germany, Japan, Spain, Switzerland, Sweden, Holland or Austria) then a different trademark may have to be chosen.

The technique of developing a worldwide trademark is very complex, but can be well worth the effort, particularly in the event of any future trademark infringement cases. If a trademark has been established on a worldwide basis, the ownership of it and rights to it are much more protectable.

Further, a worldwide trademark ensures familiarity with the brand name and with the product, as well as with the manufacturer. The combination of an innovative, worldwide trademark makes for an exceptional marketing and legal product franchise.

■ The Stages of Naming a New Drug

The brand name tends to be developed relatively late in the product's lifecycle. So before the brand name exists, there must be another way of referring to the product during its development. First the product is given a laboratory code. This is usually an alpha numeric identifier comprising initials indicating the developing laboratory and a serial number, for example, BRL (Beecham Research Labs) 54321. It is wise to keep to this convention and not to make the code name indicative of the drug under development or too 'user friendly'. Should news of the development be leaked, the company might find that everyone refers to the code number and builds up such familiarity with it that it pre-empts the role of the trademark. For example, Wellcome are still working hard to ensure people refer to Retrovir rather than AZT.

Then there is the generic name for the compound which indicates its chemical structure and sometimes indicates the broad therapy area. In each country, the generic name must be approved by an independent committee or regulatory body known as an Approved Names Committee, to ensure that it is not misleading or too similar to other generic names. The appropriate committee in the UK is known as the British Approved Names Committee (or BAN for short).

Once the generic name is fixed, a trademark can then be developed; this too will ultimately have to be approved by regulatory bodies.

■ Creating New Brand Names

The most common method employed in pharmaceutical companies which have international divisions is first to create a trademark that is acceptable to the domestic marketplace – frequently the UK or the USA – and only then, after registrability is established, will the name be checked for availability and suitability in other countries. The reasoning behind this action is simple. The USA, for example, represents about one-third of the world in terms of worldwide pharmaceutical sales, Japan represents another third, and the rest of the world represents the final third. Clearly, therefore, the USA and Japan are most likely to be the two nations which are most important to any international pharmaceutical corporation.

As has been pointed out, there are several new emerging strategies being employed in the development of international pharmaceutical trademarks and each company must decide which method is best for its situation. Many corporations have established what are known as trademark committees. These committees are made up of several members, representing various divisions of the corporation as well as various disciplines. It is the duty of the committee to recommend to upper management possible brand names for new drugs which are suitable, and which have been legally searched and found to be clear and, therefore, which are registrable all over the world. Finding a new trademark for a drug is no easy task as there are so many already registered in this class (over 40 000 in the UK alone!).

Since the task of developing a worldwide trademark is so complex, and involves considerable work, many of these committees have looked to outside agencies to develop an acceptable worldwide trademark for a specific product. These companies listen to the committee's description of a specific drug, and the corporation's intended marketing position, as well as their ideas for types of prefixes or suffixes that are preferred or disliked. The agency then conducts group panels in key cities around the world to seek the preferences of doctors and consumers. They also use computer programs to develop short lists of names for presentation to the client. Many corporations have found this method to be very satisfactory; however, the process is still quite complex, particularly when it becomes involved in the area of searching and registering trademarks in countries around the world.

As mentioned, Japan is a very significant market for international companies and, therefore, it is mandatory that a worldwide trademark be accepted in the Japanese market. Due to the great difference between Japanese and English, for example, it is advisable always to test potential names for pronunciation and use with Japanese physicians.

Another basic problem, particular to US pharmaceutical companies in developing worldwide trademarks, is that most drug products following development and clinical testing are first marketed abroad, before ever being approved in the USA. This makes the process even more complex, since the time constraints are much more severe internationally than they are in the USA. Therefore the brand name will be chosen many years in advance of the drug's approval and introduction into the US market. Agreement between the various corporate divisions (domestic and international) is often difficult to achieve in terms of a worldwide trademark but, in terms of value to a pharmaceutical corporation, it is essential to move in this direction. Zofran and Kytril are excellent examples of worldwide trademarks.

■ The Role of the Advertising Agency

As a rule advertising agencies do not enjoy developing brand names. They find the legal aspects of the process irksome and a real threat to 'creativity'; but perhaps more to the point, they rarely receive a separate fee! Agencies therefore prefer to leave name development to their clients or, as is increasingly the case these days, to specialist consultancies.

This is not to suggest that advertising agencies do not have a role to play in the development of brand names. Agencies are frequently involved at a very early stage in their clients' new product development activities and, as the new product begins to take shape and the probability that it will be launched increases, so the need arises to integrate the advertising development within the process. As the aim of the advertising will be to communicate values relevant to the new product and thus 'position' it in the marketplace in a uniquely attractive way, it is clear that the brand name and the advertising have complementary roles to play.

Ideally, therefore, the advertising agency should be involved in helping to prepare the name development brief. It may well be that their own work for the client will have included a definition of the 'personality' that the new brand should assume and information like this is critical to developing an effective naming strategy. The agency should also be involved at various points in the name development process, most particularly at the review and shortlisting stages, in order to help ensure that the names which are selected for legal searches are strategically 'on brief', and can in principle be made to work in advertising.

At the end of the day, however, it is the client and the client's branding consultancy who should make the final choice of brand name. The branding consultancy should be respected for its knowledge of brands and their crucial role in marketing; the client should be respected for having a grasp of the overall strategic objective. It is the role of the advertising agency to help bring this about – remembering always that when it comes to brands, it provides general rather than specific skills and services.

This said, there are very rarely 'tensions' between the advertising agency and brand naming consultancy. Both have the same objective in mind – the creation of a successful brand – and each has its own very specific task. Agencies occasionally feel some frustration at having to suspend creative work until the results of those tedious legal searches are known. This, however, can be avoided if all parties involved in the naming process – clients, agency and consultancy – work as a team to a mutually agreed timetable.

The Role of the Advertising Agency

- Agencies rarely enjoy brand naming – understandably, as their job is to create great advertising!
- But the name is at the heart of the brand's personality; the advertising animates this.
- The brand name and the advertising therefore have complementary roles to play.
- For the best result, the client, agency and brand naming consultancy should work together as a team.

The Role of the Design Consultancy

Little, if anything at all, has been written so far about the role of designers in helping to create brands. They too have a very specific role to play. Some of the best known brands in the world – for example, the Mercedes star, the Shell logo, McDonald's Golden Arches – are pure designs; their power lies in their distinctiveness and in their ability to surpass language barriers. But compared with the many thousands of distinctive brand names in use there are few internationally recognized brand logos with the mnemonic quality of those mentioned above.

Significantly, however, many of the world's most powerful and best-loved brands are an attractive blend of name and design. The Coca-Cola brand is a combination of four elements – the Dynamic Ribbon device, the flowing spencirian script, the trademarks Coca-Cola and Coke and the proprietary colours red and white. The Lego brand is a combination of the chunky logotype, the Lego trademark, the colour red and the 'retaining' rectangle (Image 23). The ICI name is inseparable from its roundel and stylized ocean waves. There are numerous examples of where design has been used to add distinctiveness to the brand name and thus enhance its impact and memorability. The role of the designer in the branding process therefore is to help bring the brand name to life.

It follows then that the design team must understand the positioning objectives for the new brand and must work to ensure that the structural packaging, label design and logotype are in line with these. Critically they must ensure that the creative elements of the new pack design – the use of colours, graphics and typography – complement rather than overlap with the brand name and advertising in helping to shape the desired personality for the new brand. If you doubt the importance of graphic design in helping, after the brand name, to project an enduring and engaging image of the brand, think of the

Bovis hummingbird, the Bisto kids or the placid bull wreathed in laurels that adorns the Colman's Mustard jar. All these are powerful brand symbols that far exceed in impact and longevity any advertising that may have been used to support them.

The Role of the Design Consultancy

- Design is a vital part of the branding process.
- Its role is to enhance the visual appearance of the brand name and to help build brand personality.
- Like brand name and advertising development, good design is based on firm strategic principles.
- And like brand naming and advertising, it should be treated as an integral part of the brand development process.

CHAPTER 3

How to Protect Trademarks

'I have very little notion of what the section intended to convey and particularly the sentence of 253 words which constitutes sub-section (1). I doubt if the entire statute book can be successfully researched for a sentence of equal length which is of more fuliginous obscurity.' (Lord McKinnon on the old Section 4 (1) (b) of the Trade Marks Act 1938, since amended and greatly improved!)

What Can Be Registered?

Trademark registration and legislation in the European Union has become more harmonized. The UK Trade Marks Act, which became law on 31 October 1994, is based upon the Community Trade Mark Directive which has been adopted by most of the other European Union members. Up to that point there was a significant difference in approach by European countries as to what could be registered as a trademark. In the UK the definition of a mark has been widened as a result of the new Act:

- In addition to distinctive words and designs it will now be possible to register distinctive container shapes; the distinctive shapes of the goods themselves; colours; sounds and smells as trademarks. (These are discussed in detail below.)
- It appears to be generally accepted that the distinctiveness threshold previously applied as a prerequisite to registration will be lower under the new law. This means that it will be easier to register packaging/label designs than was previously the case.
- Although under the old law it was possible to register a truly distinctive label design, it was not always easy. This was reflected in the fact that very few designs/labels had been registered and therefore the issue of trademark infringement had generally not arisen with regard to them.

This contrasts with the Benelux countries and France which traditionally had a wide definition of what could be registered as a trademark, and as a result packaging designs and labels often enjoyed the benefit of registration.

Trademark Registration – What is Now Included

Europe: Anything *represented graphically* and *capable of distinguishing* goods/services.

• words	• numbers	• colours
• designs	• shapes	• sounds
• letters	• packaging	• smells

USA: Any word, name, symbol or device used to *identify and distinguish* goods. Specifically includes get-up protection which can be registered or protected as an unregistered trademark under Section 43(a) Lanham Act.

Strong versus Weak Marks

Strong marks, which can easily be protected by way of registration, usually consist of invented words (such as Kodak, Exxon), words which have no direct meaning in relation to the goods or services (for example, Lotus for cars or Enigma for lager) or distinctive device marks such as the Black Horse logo for Lloyds Bank. By contrast weak marks often consist of words which directly refer to the character or quality of the goods, laudatory epithets, slogans, geographic names or surnames. In the past, marks which have been refused protection by way of registration include Mild for cigarettes, Have A Break for chocolate biscuits and York for trailers. Such marks are difficult to protect, especially by means of registration, because they are words other traders may wish to use when describing their goods or services. For a mark to be registrable it must be capable of distinguishing one particular trader's goods or services from those of his or her competitors.

However, under the Trade Marks Act 1994, many of these weaker marks may now be capable of registration if they have become distinctive through use. Prior to this laudatory epithets, such as Perfection, or well-known geographical place names, such as York, could never have been registered regardless of the extent of use because they were not regarded as distinctive in law.

The new Act also enables sounds and smells to be registered as trademarks, provided they can be represented graphically. Examples of sound marks are MGM's Lion's Roar for films and Direct Line Insurance's (maddening) jingle for insurance services, which are distinctive and should be capable of registration. Smells, however, are not very distinctive as trademarks, particularly for goods such as perfumes, as they are characteristic of the goods themselves and, as such, would be excluded from registration.

Three-dimensional marks such as the shape of goods or their packaging may now also be registered as trademarks. This was one of the major changes to UK trademark law introduced by the new Act and means that, for example, it has now become possible for Coca-Cola to register the shape of their bottle as a trademark whereas in the past this was held to be unregistrable. (Fittingly, the Coca-Cola 80–year old bottle design became one of the first 3–D shapes to be registered as a UK trademark, in September 1995.) However, as marks consisting of the shape of goods or their packaging are not very distinctive, applications for such marks will need to be supported by evidence showing that the mark distinguishes the proprietor's goods from those of competitors.

Colours can also serve as trademarks, provided they distinguish the proprietor's goods from those of competitors. However, as trademarks consisting merely of colours are often regarded as non-distinctive, evidence showing that they do in fact distinguish the proprietor's goods or services from those of others will usually be required. In the past, drug manufacturers have often sought registration of various colours/colour combinations for capsules or tablets; for example, SmithKline and French Laboratories Limited were successful in obtaining registration of colour combinations for capsules. Other drug manufacturers, however, have been less successful in obtaining registration of such marks – particularly if the colour(s) in question is commonly used in the pharmaceutical industry or to indicate dosage rather than to distinguish the goods. In such circumstances registration has been refused.

■ Protection

As has been discussed in earlier chapters, a trademark can become a (if not *the*) most valued and valuable property a company can own. As with any other item of valuable property, steps should be taken to protect it (see Image 29).

Essentially there are two ways of acquiring and protecting rights in a trademark: use and registration.

■ Use

□ *Passing Off*

In the UK, and other countries which have a similar legal system based on common law, rights in a trademark can be acquired through the use made of it and those rights can be protected by a legal action known as *passing off*. Essentially, the action of passing off is to protect the reputation/goodwill attributed to the trademark because of its use. It has been established over many centuries in the English Courts, that 'nobody has the right to represent his goods (*or services*) as the goods (*or services*) of somebody else'.

The essence of passing off is not to grant an automatic monopoly in a trademark, but to give legal recognition to an existing position. It is also worth noting that passing off does not necessarily have to involve merely the unauthorized use of a trademark, but can include unauthorized use of a similar get up (such as packaging), indeed anything that could be said to 'represent' one person's goods (*or services*) as the goods (*or services*) of somebody else.

A passing off action is a bit like a cake, in that it has to consist of certain ingredients for it to be successful. Those ingredients are:

- A reputation acquired through use.
- A misrepresentation.
- Confusion (or likelihood of confusion).
- Damage (or likelihood of damage).

As with a cake, if an ingredient is missing the cake is a failure, so too with an action for passing off. If any of the above ingredients is missing the action will fail.

□ *Unfair Competition*

Some common law countries (for example the USA) but more usually those countries that have a civil code legal system (for example most continental European countries) have a similar concept to passing off, known as ***unfair** competition.*

By its very definition, the action for unfair competition is to remedy unfairness, and can be somewhat wider in application than a passing off action. The UK does not generally recognize unfair competition concepts as such. An unfair competition action, for example, would probably be taken by the proprietor of a very well-known mark (for example Kodak, Coke, Rolls-Royce) if the mark, or something confusingly similar to it was used by an unauthorized third party, in relation to goods or services which are not necessarily associated with the famous mark (for example unauthorized use of Kodak as a trademark for televisions).

■ Registration – Infringement

The second means of acquiring and protecting rights in a trademark is by registering the trademark on the Trade Marks Register in a particular territory.

Once a trademark is registered, the registered proprietor of the mark is given the exclusive right to use the mark in relation to the goods or services claimed by the registration and in many territories, this will extend to similar goods or services and in certain circumstances even to unrelated goods or services. The registered proprietor can bring a legal action called trademark *infringement* to prevent the unauthorized use of the registered trademark, or a confusingly similar trademark, on the basis that the statutory monopoly has been breached.

The same remedies are available in an infringement action as they are for passing off (for example, injunction and damages) and the practical implication and conditions of such actions are covered in the next chapter – Trademark Management. The availability of protection in Europe and the USA is summarized in Table 3.1.

Why Register?

As mentioned above, registration provides the best form of protection for a trademark for the following reasons.

- **Monopoly rights.** The registered proprietor of a registered trademark is given the statutory monopoly to use of that trademark in relation to the goods or services claimed by it (and in many countries, similar goods or services) and can prevent the unauthorized use of the registered trademark, or a confusingly similar trademark, by a third party.
- **Easier enforcement.** Because registration grants a statutory monopoly, once a third party is threatened with an action for trademark infringement, it is taken far more seriously, as the argument is simply a question of fact: is the trademark which is being used a confusingly similar trademark to the registered trademark and is such use on the same or similar goods or services? If it is, then infringement has occurred.
- **Use is not a prerequisite.** Unlike passing off, the Plaintiff (the party bringing the legal action) does not have to establish a reputation through

Table 3.1 The Availability of Protection

Country	*Passing off*	*Unfair competition**	*Trademark infringement*	*Specific trade dress and get up protection*
UK	✓	✗	✓	✗
'Benelux'	✗	✓	✓	✗
France	✗	✓	✓	✗
Spain	✗	✓	✓	✗
Germany	✗	✓	✓	✓
Italy	✗	✓	✓	✗
Denmark	✗	✓	✓	✓
Sweden	✗	✓	✓	✗
USA	✓	✓	✓	✓

* Includes fair trading legislation

use of the registered trademark. Indeed, the registered proprietor of a registered trademark does not even have to use the registered trademark to bring an infringement action. It is worth pointing out, however, that if a registered trademark remains unused after it has become registered for a given period (ranging from country to country, usually between three and five years) it can be cancelled for non-use, and this should be borne in mind before proceeding with an infringement action.

- **More cost effective.** As no reputation has to be proved, nor indeed do actual instances of confusion or damage have to be shown (unlike passing off), an infringement action is often much cheaper to bring than a passing off action. There is nothing to prevent a trademark owner from bringing both actions at the same time.
- **Unlimited life.** The statutory monopoly conferred by registration can have an unlimited life, provided the trademark registration is renewed, and it does not become vulnerable to cancellation for non-use.
- **The deterrent factor.** Once a trademark is placed on the Trade Marks Register, a public record of the registered proprietors' interest in the mark is created and can serve as a 'keep off the grass' notice to competitors thinking of adopting a similar mark.
- **Status of unregistered rights.** This is discussed in more detail below. However it is worth pointing out that in the UK it is possible that if a trademark is used but not registered, a third party, if it succeeded in registering the trademark, could prevent the further use of the earlier used unregistered trademark, or at least prevent the extension of such use.

Additionally, some countries – for example, Spain – do not recognize unregistered rights – perhaps with the exception of unregistered well-known trademarks.

■ Registration Practices

As has been identified, the registration of a trademark is something worth striving for. However, not all trademarks will be registrable. This is because the result of a registration (that is, the granting of a statutory monopoly) is very serious, and it would be unfair to grant any one particular party a statutory monopoly in something that should be freely available for others to use (for example, descriptive words).

There are two types of registration practice adopted by those countries which allow for the registration of trademarks (most countries of the world). Those which have an examination procedure, and those which do not (a few countries, for example, France).

Examination

Examination tends to come in one or both of two forms known as 'absolute' and 'relative'.

- **Absolute** This involves the trademark which has been applied for registration being examined as to whether it is acceptable to be granted monopoly rights. For example, is it descriptive, or deceptive, or laudatory, or the simple shape of the product, or a geographical location etc? Essentially the test will be, is it fair to grant the applicant a monopoly in the trademark?

  Countries which adopt an absolute examination procedure include the UK, USA, Japan, Germany and most common law countries.
- **Relative** This involves the Trade Mark Registries conducting a search of their Trade Mark Registers to see if there are any prior registrations or applications already on file which conflict with the mark that has been applied for. Rules of comparison of trademarks will vary from country to country, but generally will involve visual, phonetical and conceptual considerations. For example, it is to be remembered that two conflicting trademarks may not necessarily appear side by side in the market place, and that consumers can have an imperfect recollection. In the pharmaceutical industry, however, with doctors' handwriting being notoriously illegible, far greater care is exercised when comparing pharmaceutical trademarks.

  Countries which adopt a relative examination procedure include the UK, the USA, Japan, Spain, Scandinavian countries and most common law countries.

Most countries adopt both examination procedures. Such countries include the UK, USA, Japan, the Scandinavian countries and most common law countries. Interestingly, Germany only adopts an absolute examination procedure, and leaves it to the registered proprietors of trademarks to oppose applications if they believe they conflict with their existing registration(s).

Deposit System

Countries which have no examination procedures are known as deposit countries, simply because the applications to register the trademarks are deposited on the trademark registers without any examination (either on absolute or relative grounds) being conducted. The concept behind this is that the registry is simply there to register trademarks, and any conflict should be resolved in the courts. It is usually the proprietor of the earliest valid registered trademark who is in the strongest position to prevent the use of later filed registrations. Countries which adopt such a system include France, Austria, the Benelux countries and Italy.

Table 3.2 gives a summary of examination systems.

Table 3.2 Examination Systems

Country	*System used*
Denmark	Partial Examination
UK	Full Examination
France	No Examination
Germany	Partial Examination
'Benelux'	No Examination
Spain	Full Examination
Italy	No Examination
Denmark	Full Examination
Sweden	Full Examination
USA	Full Examination

Notes:
Full examination: 'Absolute' and 'relative' assessment
Partial Examination: 'Absolute' assessment only
No Examination: The 'deposit' system

■ Conducting a Trademark Availability Search

Before registering a trademark and more importantly, before using a trademark, a clearance search **must** be conducted, to avoid being on the wrong end of a court injunction demanding the withdrawal of the product or service from the market place; this can obviously be an extremely expensive exercise on top of probably having to pay damages as well!

■ What to Search?

When conducting a trademark clearance search, obviously the trademark registers should be searched and in many cases, also the corresponding register of company names. In those countries which recognize unregistered trademark rights acquired through use, relevant trade directories should also be searched. In particular product areas (such as pharmaceuticals), there are 'in use' data bases available which should also be checked. In practice however, most conflicts will be located on the trademarks registers.

■ Develop a Sensible Strategy

Do not bank on your favourite name being available. In today's complex world, the trademark registers are becoming increasingly congested (particularly in the pharmaceuticals and electrical products areas). You should ideally start with a shortlist of names, all of which meet your marketing requirements, and be prepared to go with any that survive the legal screening.

The number of names to begin with will depend on the product area and also the number of territories which it is intended to use the mark.

It is often worthwhile conducting an identical screening of the relevant trademark registers. Identical trademark searches are a relatively inexpensive way of eliminating marks which have already been adopted.

■ Timing/Costs

From a UK perspective, trademark searches can be conducted within a matter of hours, but usually you should allow for one working week. Costs will vary from £200 to £250 per mark (assuming that only one class is involved). If additional classes are involved, then the cost will increase between 10 per cent and 20 per cent for each additional class.

Non-UK searches tend to be more expensive and you should budget for approximately £400 per mark per territory. This is again based on only one class being involved and the same 10–20 per cent extra per class should be budgeted for if additional classes are involved.

As far as timing is concerned, as already mentioned, a full search of the UK Trade Marks Register can be conducted within a matter of hours, although will usually be between three and five working days. Non-UK searches can be conducted within a week (or quicker), but generally you should allow for two to three weeks.

The more urgent the search turnaround time, the greater the price premium that will be levied by the trademark attorney/searcher.

■ Unscrambling

As stated, do not expect your favourite mark to be available. Indeed, it is becoming increasingly the case that searches reveal problems that on paper are serious conflicts, but with a little further investigating (for example, investigating whether they have been used or not) could be unscrambled, for example, either by threatening a cancellation action in order to secure a Letter of Consent, or even purchasing the conflicting mark concerned. Time should, therefore, be built into your programmes to allow for possible unscrambling. If approaches have to be made to the proprietors of conflicting marks for consent, the replies may not be forthcoming for a month or two.

■ Timing

Do not leave trademark searches to the last minute, because you are more than likely to encounter a problem in the searching exercise. Certainly, do not commit yourself to any major expense (such as promotional literature being printed) until legal clearance of the mark has been given.

US Patents and Trade Marks Office (USPTO)

As the USA is an important market for most companies, it is useful to have a separate section to highlight one or two peculiarities involved in registering trademarks there.

Basis for Registration

In most countries, applications to register trademarks are filed on the basis that the mark is either in use, or the owner has a bona fide intention to use the mark. This is also the case in the USA and one or other of these bases has to be stated on the application form. Before a Certificate of Registration is issued, however, the trademark owner will be required to prove to the USPTO that the mark has been put into use in commerce in the United States, or between the United States and an overseas country.

A way around having to prove such use before registration is granted is available to overseas applicants. They can base their application on an intention to use the mark in combination with the fact that the mark is registered (or applied for) in an overseas country. Even though the application is based on an intention to use, as long as the applicant can provide a certified copy of the Certificate of Registration in the overseas country, registration in the USA will be granted.

Claims of Goods/Services

The USPTO is particularly strict in not allowing applications to claim wide specifications of goods/services and will also object to phrases that are too vague. Applications will therefore usually be quite specific in the claims made.

Signatory of the Application Form

Application forms filed at the USPTO must be signed by a duly authorized officer of the company, usually a vice president or, in the case of UK companies, a company director or the company secretary. (An example of a US trademark application form is shown in the Appendix.)

Federal versus State Registrations

Ordinarily, an application to register a trademark will be made on the Federal Trade Marks Register, thus providing protection throughout the USA. It would therefore seem inappropriate to apply for separate state registrations. However, it is possible to register a trademark in an individual state and this would apply if the trademark owner required only limited geographic protection, if it only used the mark in one state, or if its application to the Federal Register failed for some reason. Additionally, in a few states, a state registration will also provide particular rights and remedies which are helpful in that particular state (for example California).

Supplemental Register

The Federal Register consists of a principal register and a supplemental register. Those marks which are not considered sufficiently distinctive to qualify for registration on the principal register may qualify for registration on the supplemental register. By its definition, the supplemental register does not provide the trademark owner with as strong a protection for the mark as it would if it were registered on the principal register. In effect, it perhaps simply provides a form of 'deterrent notice' to unauthorized users of that mark or a confusingly similar mark.

Use of the ® Symbol

The ® is the universally recognized symbol for a registered trademark and in many countries the use of this symbol is not compulsory. If a trademark is unregistered, the ™ symbol is used. In the USA, however, it is extremely important to indicate (for example on packaging or promotional literature) that a trademark is registered at the United States Patent and Trademark Office (USPTO). To fail to do so would affect the remedies available to the registered proprietor in an infringement action (for example, it could improve the chances of collecting damages against the infringer). However, not using the ® symbol should not affect the ability to obtain an injunction to prevent unauthorized use. Certainly, not using the ® symbol will not affect a claim to ownership of the mark. It is simply to put 'the world' on notice of the fact that the mark is registered at the USPTO. It is also sometimes useful to use the following wording on packaging/literature: 'Reg. US Pat. & TM Off'.

Post Registration Matters

Between the fifth and sixth years from the date of registration, a declaration (affidavit) has to be filed at the USPTO by the trademark owner confirming that the mark is in use or has been in continuous use for five consecutive years from the date of registration and that the mark is still in use. If this declaration is not filed, the registration is invalidated. These are known as Section 8 and Section 15 affidavits.

The requirement of the Section 8 affidavit is to inform the USPTO that the mark is in use, and that your registration should continue in force (although the use may not have been continuous from the date of registration).

The Section 15 affidavit confirms the same, but also informs the PTO that the mark has been in continuous use since it was registered, and the proprietor is

Image 1 The Coca-Cola logo

Image 2 'It's the real thing'

The Coca-Cola trademarks include the name, its distinctive logo style, the 'Dynamic Ribbon device', the highly distinctive contour bottle, many of the company's slogans (such as 'It's the real thing') and also its distinctive combination of colours

(Coca-Cola, Coke, the Dynamic Ribbon device and the design of the contour bottle are registered trademarks of The Coca-Cola Company. These trademarks are reproduced with kind permission of The Coca-Cola Company.)

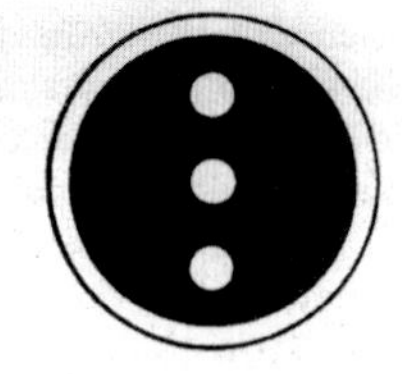

Image 3
The mark of the potter who made Etruscan vases

Image 4
The symbol of the mighty Habsburg Empire which dominated Europe for hundreds of years

Image 5 Quaker
The beaming Quaker – a product of the latter part of the industrial revolution

Image 6 Whitbread Hind's head
The modern use of a heraldic device as a trademark

Image 7 Manet's painting *Bar at the Folies Bergères*

Image 8 The Bass logo
The first registered trademark in the UK

Image 9 Exxon
The name is a pure invention – one of the strongest forms of trademark

Image 10 Michelin
The pneumatic Monsieur Bibendum is a powerful 'suggestive' trademark

Image 11 Kwik-Fit
Powerfully descriptive – a communication strength but a legal weakness

Image 12 4711
The well-known eau de Cologne: an interesting mark – but numbers are sometimes difficult to protect

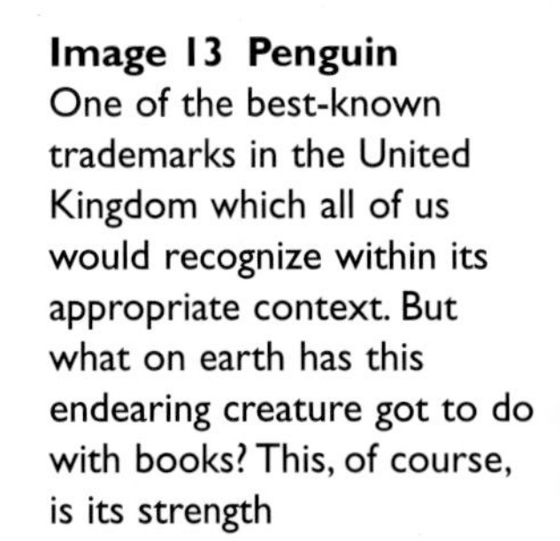

Image 13 Penguin
One of the best-known trademarks in the United Kingdom which all of us would recognize within its appropriate context. But what on earth has this endearing creature got to do with books? This, of course, is its strength

Image 14 Visa logo
Something that permits you freedom of access – to a country and to cash and other financial services: a brilliant association of ideas

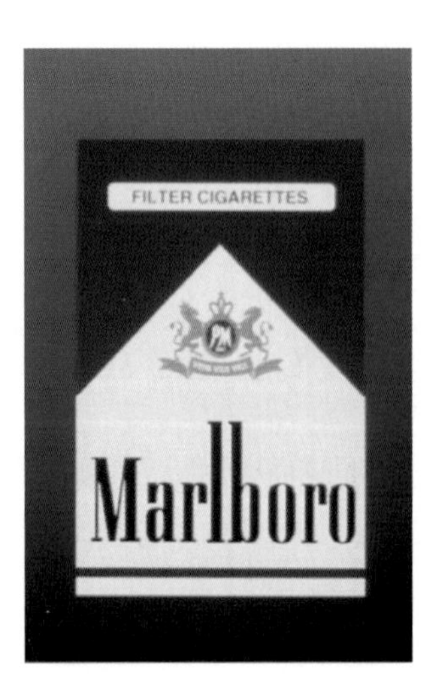

Image 15 Marlboro Logo
Valued recently at $40 bn

Bimbo Bread

Nora Knackers

Kräpp Toilet Paper

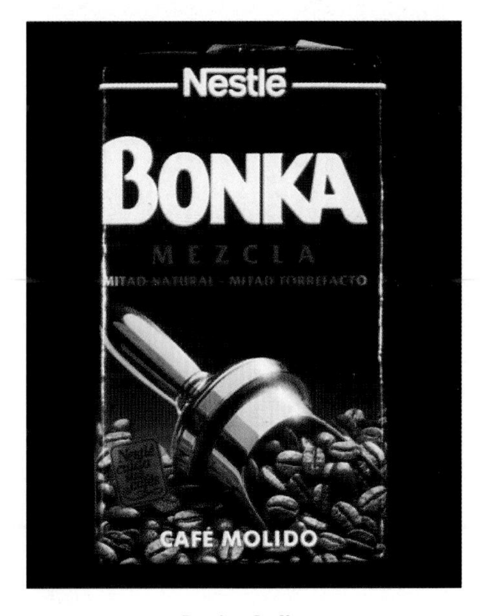

Bonka Coffee

Images 16–19

A gallery of bizarre (to English speakers) brand names. Ironically each was conceived in complete innocence by its owner. There is little doubt that the names coined have simple functionality – but none of the brands was intended to travel!

Image 20 The Lego® logo
The famous Lego trademark has moved with the times – just like the products it represents. No radical changes have been made but there have been gradual and logical adjustments leading to the trademark which is so well known today.
(®Lego and the Lego logo are registered trademarks of the Lego Group.)

Image 21 The Bovis hummingbird

Image 22 The Colman's bull

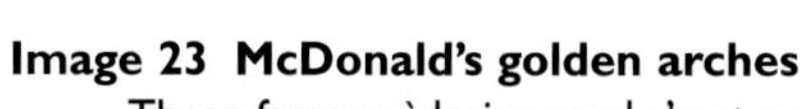

Image 23 McDonald's golden arches
These famous `design marks' act as powerful mnemonics for their brands

Image 24 Levi's
A brand that is treasured as a symbol of western culture

Image 25 The Kodak logo
The Kodak brand name and logo are protected throughout the world by trademark registrations. Certain features of the packaging will be protected by registered designs. The technical manuals, original drawings and advertising materials are protected by copyright – as will the logo. And certain of the machines and processes will be protected by patents

Image 26 BP logo

Image 27 Red Funnel logo

Image 28 Classic Cola and Coca-Cola

'Lookalikes' are retailer private label brands which mimic the trade dress of the brand leader. Their purpose is to compete by unfair means with brands where conventional, fair, private label tactics have failed

therefore now claiming 'incontestability status' for the mark. Essentially, 'incontestability status' will make it extremely difficult (although not necessarily impossible) for a third party to challenge the validity of your registration. This does not affect a third party claiming that after a Section 15 affidavit has been filed, the mark ceased to continue to be in use, and it could therefore be cancelled for such non-use.

■ Filing an Application

If the results of an availability search reveal that a mark is available for usc and registration, it is advisable to file an application for registration as soon as possible.

■ The UK

An application is made by filing the relevant form at the Patent Office and paying the appropriate fee. The application must include the following information:

- a request for registration of the trademark
- the name and address of the applicant
- a statement of the goods or services in relation to which it is sought to register the trademark
- a representation of the trademark
- a statement that the trademark is being used by the applicant or with his or her consent in relation to the goods or services claimed, or that he or she has a bona fide intention that it should be so used.

The application will not be given a filing date until all this information has been provided.

The statement of the goods or services must not be too wide and claims for all goods in a particular class are not acceptable. It is possible to cover goods or services falling in more than one class on payment of an additional fee. If the mark applied for is a three-dimensional mark, sound or smell it must be represented graphically on the application form. The statement that the trademark is being used by the applicant or that the applicant has a bona fide intention to use the mark is required to ensure that applications are not filed in bad faith.

■ Overseas

The application procedure in other countries is very similar, although it is usually necessary to appoint a trademark attorney in the relevant country. In most cases all that is required is a power of attorney, simply signed by an authorized signatory of the applicant company. Sometimes however this document must be notarised and/or legalized. The trademark attorney acting on behalf of the applicants will also require a representation of the trademark, a list of the goods or services for which protection is sought and the name, address and nationality of the applicant. In some countries it is possible, as in the UK, to file multi-class applications; in others it is necessary to file a separate application in each class of interest.

Costs and Further Bureaucratic Procedures

Although recently there has been an attempt to harmonize trademark legislation in the European Union, costs and procedures still differ here and throughout the world – often widely.

The UK

In the UK the government fee for filing one trademark application in one class is £225. Additional classes can be included in the same application at a cost of £50 per class. If the applicant instructs a firm of trademark attorneys to file the application on his behalf, they will usually charge a set fee (approximately £220 for one trademark in one class).

A few months after the application has been filed it will be officially examined by the Registrar of Trade Marks to ensure that it meets all the statutory requirements for registration. The registrar may raise objections to the application if the mark is descriptive, deceptive or contrary to law or public policy. The registrar also carries out a search of the register for conflicting marks and will raise an objection if the mark conflicts with an earlier registration of the identical or similar mark covering the same or similar goods or services. The registrar will advise the applicant of any objections to the application and will allow a period of six months for the applicant to respond, for example by filing written submissions arguing for acceptance of the mark or by submitting evidence of use. If the arguments submitted are unsuccessful, the applicant has the right to apply for a Hearing at the Trade Marks Registry, at which to argue the case further before a more senior official.

If no objections are raised or if the applicant is eventually successful in overcoming any objections which are raised to the application, it will be advertised in the *Trade Marks Journal* for opposition purposes. A period of three months is allowed for third parties to oppose the application and no extension of this term is possible. This three-month period is intended to allow the parties time to negotiate to see if they can reach an amicable settlement before formal opposition proceedings are launched, as such proceedings can be time consuming and expensive. Alternatively, once an application is advertised, a third party is entitled to make observations in writing to the Registrar as to whether the trademark should be registered.

Provided no oppositions are filed within the three month period the application should proceed to registration and the registration certificate will be issued. Once registered, rights in the mark are backdated to the date of filing the application and the period of registration runs for 10 years from the date of filing the application. The registration can then be renewed indefinitely for further periods of 10 years.

If an applicant instructs a firm of trademark attorneys to prosecute the application this will involve additional costs, usually charged on a time basis. The extent of these charges will depend on the nature of any official or third-party objections which arise; however, if the application is fairly straightforward they are normally in the region of £200–£300. On the other hand, if formal opposition proceedings are entered into, costs could be as high as £3000 plus counsel's fees.

■ Overseas

The registration procedure varies from country to country, as does the time involved. In many countries, such as the USA, Japan, South Africa, Australia and New Zealand, the procedure is similar to that in the UK in that applications are officially examined and advertised for opposition purposes. Other countries, such as 'the Benelux' (which includes the Netherlands, Belgium and Luxembourg for the purposes of obtaining trademark registration), France and Italy operate what is known as a 'deposit' system whereby applications are filed and proceed to registration without a full official examination being undertaken.

Table 3.3 shows the average time from application to registration in the USA and Europe.

Table 3.3 How Long Does It Take to Register?

Country	*Average time from application to registration*
UK	1–2 years
France	under 3 months
Germany	1 year
'Benelux'	3–6 months
Spain	2–4 years
Italy	2–4 years
Denmark	1–2 years
Sweden	1–2 years
USA	1 year

The Trademark Attorney

Trademark attorneys play an important role in the clearing and registration of trademarks because they are qualified experts in this complex field. As far as clearance of trademarks is concerned, they can carry out availability searches, use investigations worldwide and handle third-party negotiations. They can assist in the registration process, handle third-party conflicts, assist with licensing and assignments and provide advice on correct usage of trademarks.

In matters of trademark protection, or in pursuing an application for registration, a skilled and determined trademark attorney is worth his – or equally her – weight in gold. Their status in many countries is ambiguous; in the UK, for example, they comprise a separate profession whereas in many others, they are qualified lawyers specializing in this area. As guardians of a business's most precious assets they are vital members of the brand management team. The cost of their services is exceptionally modest in relation to the value they supply.

Importance of Usage

In the UK, a registration becomes vulnerable to cancellation for non-use if there has been no use of the mark, by the proprietor or with his or her consent, for five years from the date the registration was entered on the register in relation to the goods or services for which it is registered, or if use has been suspended for an uninterrupted period of five years or longer.

Following the implementation of the Trade Marks Act 1994, the onus is now on the proprietor to prove use of the mark in revocation proceedings (under the old Act the onus was on the applicant for rectification to prove that there had not been any use of the mark during the relevant period). Therefore, it is now easier and cheaper for interested parties to apply for cancellation of a registration.

A period of three months is allowed to enable the parties to enter into negotiations with a view to resolving the matter on an amicable basis. Any use during the three-month period prior to filing the application for revocation will be disregarded provided the proprietor has been informed of the intention to apply for revocation.

Use can be by the proprietor or with the proprietor's consent, which means that use by an unregistered licensee would be sufficient to save a registration from cancellation on the grounds of non-use.

It is also important to ensure that the trademark does not become the generic name in the trade for the product or service for which it is registered as this could result in rights in the mark being lost.

International Classification System

The goods and services for which trademark registration can be obtained are divided into 42 classes known as the International Classification of Goods and Services. Brief details of the types of goods and services proper to each class are shown in the Appendix.

Most countries adhere to the International Classification system and when filing a trademark application it is necessary to list the goods and services for which protection is required and to designate the appropriate classes. In the UK, the USA and most of Western Europe it is possible to cover more than one class of goods and services in the same application on payment of additional fees. However, there are still many countries throughout the world (for example, Spain) where a separate application is required for each class, thereby considerably increasing the costs of filing and prosecuting the applications.

In countries which do not follow the International Classification system, such as Brazil and Taiwan, it is necessary to classify the relevant goods and services according to the local classification system. It is also worth noting that there is no classification system whatsoever in Canada, although the Canadian trademark authorities insist that specifications of goods and services are not overly broad in scope.

Developments in the EU – The Community Trademark

The Community Trade Mark (CTM) system has been in the pipeline since 1964 when it was first proposed by the European Commission. However, an EU Regulation for the Community Trade Mark was not eventually finalized until 1993. The Community Trade Marks Office (OHIM), based in Alicante, Spain, started accepting applications from 1 January 1996 and the system officially started on 1 April 1996, with applications filed during the period 1 January to 31 March 1996 being given an effective filing date of 1 April 1996.

The purpose of the CTM system is to establish a single trademark registration covering all the member states of the EU. However, the CTM will not replace existing national registrations, which will continue in parallel.

Applications to register a CTM can be filed either direct through OHIM or at any one of the national trademark registries. Applications can be filed in any of the official languages of the EU although the working languages for the OHIM are English, French, German, Italian and Spanish. Applicants are also required to designate a second language being one of the five working languages of the OHIM.

The registration procedure involves official examination of the application to see whether the trademark is registrable. The criteria which apply are effectively the same as the 'absolute' grounds for refusal under the UK Trade Marks Act, 1994 (see p. 52).

OHIM also carries out an official search of the Community Trade Marks Register and draws the applicant's attention to any prior marks which appear to conflict. However, an application will not be refused based on the results of the official search and the onus is therefore on the applicant to decide whether or not to proceed, bearing in mind that the owners of conflicting marks will be able to oppose the application. Similar searches will also be carried out in the national registers of all EU countries (except France, Germany and Italy). Again, however, the application will not be rejected on the grounds of conflict with any prior marks found and those marks will merely be drawn to the applicant's attention.

Once accepted, a CTM application will be published for opposition purposes and there will be a period of three months from the date of publication within which interested third parties may raise objection. In the absence of oppositions, the application will then proceed to registration for an initial period of 10 years, renewable indefinitely for further 10 year periods.

In the case of a trademark which is available throughout the EU, the CTM system is a simple and cost-effective way of obtaining a registration applicable in all member states. However, in practice – given that the registers in all member states are very crowded – it seems likely that many CTM applications will encounter third-party oppositions, other than in the case of well-known trademarks already covered by existing national registrations. It is therefore worth noting that when a pending application is refused or successfully opposed, the applicant has the option of applying to convert the application to separate national applications, clearly an attractive feature of the system.

The Madrid Arrangement and the Madrid Protocol

The Madrid Arrangement for the International Registration of Trade Marks, known as the Madrid Agreement, has provided an international registration system since 1891. An applicant, which should be a national of a member country or have a real and effective commercial establishment in a member country, first obtains registration in its home country and then applies to the World Intellectual Property Organization (WIPO) in Geneva for an international registration by designating the member states in which protection is required. The application is then sent to the national office in each designated country, which examines and prosecutes the application according to its national laws. The outcome is an international registration covering a number of countries, which is obtained more quickly and cost-effectively than filing separate national applications in the countries concerned.

Although the Madrid Arrangement has worked very well over a considerable period of time, important countries such as the USA, Japan and the UK have not joined, for the following reasons:

- The Madrid Agreement requires an international registration to be based on a national registration which puts these countries at an immediate disadvantage because of the length of time normally taken to obtain registration.
- The Agreement includes provisions for 'central attack' whereby the international registration is dependent upon the national registration on which it is based for the first five years, during which time if the national registration is cancelled, the entire International registration is also cancelled.
- The national trademark offices are required to notify WIPO of objections to international registrations within a period of twelve months, considered to be too short a timescale.
- The fees payable to national registries for handling Madrid Arrangement applications are considered to be too low.

The Madrid Protocol of 1989, technically a modification of the Madrid Agreement, is a parallel system which provides for the international registration of trademarks and is intended to attract those countries for which the original Madrid Agreement was unacceptable. However, the Protocol is different from the original Madrid Agreement in the following ways:

- Protocol applications can be based on national applications rather than national registrations.
- Central attack will no longer apply.
- National trademark registries will have up to eighteen months to examine applications and notify WIPO of objections.
- The fees will be higher and are expected to be equal to national application fees in the relevant countries.

A further advantage of the Protocol over the Madrid Agreement for English speaking countries is that the official language of the original Agreement was French, whereas under the Protocol applications may be made in either English or French.

The Madrid Protocol came into force on 1 January 1996. The following countries have so far joined: UK, Germany, China, Cuba, Norway, Sweden, Finland, Denmark, Poland, Spain, Czech Republic, Monaco and North Korea.

It follows that applicants in some countries now have the option of applying for registration of trademarks through their national trademarks office, via the Community Trade Mark system, The Madrid Arrangement or The Madrid Protocol. It will depend on the particular circumstances of each individual case as to which route is appropriate.

Unregistered Trademarks

In countries such as the UK and the USA where rights to a trademark can be acquired through use as well as by registration it is important when choosing a new trademark to ensure that it does not conflict with unregistered or registered prior marks.

While it is relatively straightforward to conduct a search of the Trade Marks Register, common law searches tend to provide less reliable results. For example, the difficulties of trying to establish whether there are conflicting marks in use in an unregistered capacity in a country as large as the USA are obvious. None the less it is important to check information sources such as telephone and telefax directories, trade directories, company name registers and on-line databases to ensure that there are no likely problems. If these searches indicate that the same or similar mark is in use, it is necessary to investigate further to establish whether there is a real risk of conflict, bearing in mind that common law rights can form a valid basis for objection to use or registration of a later mark.

Unregistered rights are always the most difficult to protect. Like a boxer forced onto the ropes, or a batsman who can only play fast bowling off the back foot, successfully 'seeing off' the opposition is mightily difficult; one is always in a position of relative weakness. Registered rights, on the other hand, can provide that knockout punch or devastating drive, scattering the opposition – infringers – left, right and centre.

Corporate Names

It is a commonly held misconception that by incorporating a company in the UK, the proprietor acquires rights in the name and can prevent its unauthorized use by third parties. In fact incorporation of a company does not provide any rights in the name *per se*, although it does mean that the Registrar of Companies will refuse to incorporate another company under the identical name. It is possible, however that use of a company name could conflict with existing common law rights and lead to an objection on the grounds of passing off.

In the past, use of a full company name was a defence to an action for trademark infringement in the UK, although this no longer applies under the Trade Marks Act 1994. Therefore when incorporating a new company or choosing a trademark it is necessary to check the Companies Register to ensure that there are no likely obstacles.

The law relating to company names and the extent to which incorporating a company name provides rights in the name differ substantially from country to country. It is therefore advisable to obtain specialist local advice on searching procedures, how to incorporate in the relevant country and the rights, if any, that incorporation of a company provides.

CHAPTER 4

Trademark Management

Main Principles of Trademark Management

For any company that relies upon its trademarks to provide its products or services with a competitive advantage, the main principles of trademark management are simple.

1. Ensure that everyone within the organization – in the departments responsible for production, marketing, finance, logistics and so on – understands and acknowledges that your trademarks are valuable and important assets.
2. Take full advantage of the provisions which exist under law in all current and potential countries of interest to protect your trademarks.
3. Abide by the 'five golden rules' (p. 60) for good trademark usage and insist that everyone within the organization understands and applies these according to the procedures described in your trademarks manual.
4. Seek the very best trademark advice in all countries where you intend to market your goods or services. Retain experts in trademark law, not generalists.
5. Move swiftly and ruthlessly against any third party whose activities may threaten your trademark rights.

Adherence to these principles will help preserve the value and potency of these most precious corporate assets. And each of these is elaborated on in the following pages.

Main Principles of Trademark Management

1. Your company's trademarks are valuable and important assets.
2. Use the protection that is available to you in law.
3. Apply the 'five golden rules'.
4. For peace of mind, retain a trademark lawyer.
5. Move swiftly and ruthlessly against infringers!

Correct Usage is Essential

In some countries of the world, a trademark becomes the legal property of the person first using it, and exclusive rights are acquired in a mark from the moment of that first use. In many other countries, however, the first person to register a mark obtains the rights in it, sometimes regardless of any prior or subsequent use. Registration invariably confers stronger rights than use; it is far simpler to sue for infringement of a trademark registration than it is to bring an action either for passing off or for unfair competition (either of which can be based only on use or reputation). It should therefore be the policy of the trademark owner to register, or at least attempt to register, all of its marks.

A trademark registration gives its owner the right to sue for infringement anyone who uses the same or confusingly similar mark on any of the goods or services for which the mark is registered (often, as is now the case in the United Kingdom, for confusingly similar goods and services too). But the rights acquired by registration, and the rights that go with it, can be lost if a trademark is not used correctly. Some words now in everyday use started off their lives as trademarks (for example gramophone, zip, tabloid and escalator), and others, while still registered marks, are frequently thought of by the public as being common names (for example Biro, Thermos, Cellophane). Hard work and constant vigilance by the trademark owner is required to ensure that marks in the latter category remain validly registered and immune from use by third parties.

Correct Usage is Essential

- Registration confers powerful rights of monopoly upon the trademark owner.
- Such rights can be eroded, however, by careless misuse – zip, tabloid, escalator and gramophone were all once registered trademarks but their owners failed to protect or use them correctly.

Five Golden Rules

The following are cardinal rules for the use of trademarks:

Rule One: Always use a trademark as an adjective

A trademark is an adjective. It is not a noun and it is not a verb. It should always be used in print as an adjective qualifying a noun or noun phrase. The noun or noun phrase which the trademark adjective must qualify is of course the generic name for the product.

- **Incorrect use**

  Fit a Velux in your loft.

  Treat yourself to a Hob-Nob.

- **Correct Use**

  Fit a Velux roof window in your loft.

  Treat yourself to a Hob-Nobs biscuit.

The correct grammatical treatment is frequently overlooked; it is bad trademark practice and, more importantly, damages the mark itself.

■ Rule Two: Do not use plurals or possessives

A trademark, being an adjective, must not appear in the plural or possessive sense.

- **Incorrect use**

  All Kit-Kats are made from the finest ingredients.

  Mercedes' unique new braking system.

- **Correct use**

  Kit-Kat biscuits are made from the finest ingredients.

  The unique new braking system in Mercedes cars.

■ Rule Three: Always use a trademark with a generic term

A trademark must always be used in print close to a generic word or phrase which describes the product, for example:

Quorn, a versatile alternative to meat
The engine oils Mobil 1 and Mobil Super XHP
McDougall's self-raising flour
Guinness stout
American Express, the world's leading charge card service
Thermos, the original vacuum flask
Cuprinol wood preservatives

Provided the trademark is used in this fashion, then it is apparent to the reader that the mark is not the only word by which the product or service is known and the supplier of a competitive product does not have to use the trademark to describe his own product. Trademarks such as Hoover, Formica and Xerox are often wrongly used by the public in this sense. Used correctly, there is no risk that the mark can go the way of words such as zip or gramophone and become the generic name for the goods. This is especially important for patented new products which, for much of their lives, often have no direct competitor. Therefore a product must also have a generic name which should be coined when the product is first marketed, and subsequently used consistently throughout its life – for to change the generic descriptor after a period of time is confusing to the purchaser and damaging to the trademark.

In printed matter, a mark ideally should be followed by its generic name; but this can make for cumbersome reading (Micron antifouling paint, Tampax tampons, Duracell alkaline batteries). Therefore it is an acceptable compromise to print the mark plus its generic descriptor at an early stage in the copy, perhaps in the heading or when it is first shown and subsequently to use either the mark or the generic alone.

■ Rule Four: Indicate a trademark clearly in print

The most powerful trademarks are those which are distinctive. It is appropriate therefore that the trademark should be treated distinctively in print in such a way that the reader is put on notice that the word is a trademark – otherwise the reader will not know that the word is a trademark and may be tempted to misuse it. There are numerous ways of indicating that a word is a trademark, for example:

- Quotation marks – 'Hamlet' cigar.
- Capital letters – ZOVIRAX anti-herpetic cream.
- Different typeface – *Penguin* paperbacks.
- Heavy type – **Smirnoff** vodka.
- Colour – Kodak trade dress yellow (see Image 25).
- Footnote – an asterisk beside the mark and then '*trademark' at the end of the copy.
- A symbol – ® or ™ (see below).
- Words – Levi's trademark (see Image 24).

■ Rule Five: Use the word 'registered'

It is generally acceptable to use the ® symbol to indicate that a word or device is a trademark. In many countries however this symbol usually has the legal meaning of 'registered trademark' and since there are very few countries in the world which do not have penalties for describing a mark as registered when it is not – and since it is sometimes difficult to achieve registration of a company's trademarks in all countries of interest – it would be wise to avoid the use of the word 'registered' or the ® symbol for products destined for many markets, unless the trademark is at least registered in the country of origin. An acceptable alternative, often used in the USA, while the trademark application is still pending, is to use ™. It should also be noted that in some countries it is essential to indicate that a mark is registered in order to be able to assert one's rights subsequently against third parties. In the USA, for example, the ® symbol must be used as soon as the mark is registered, as otherwise it is not possible to obtain damages in infringement proceedings.

Five Golden Rules

1. Always use the trademark as an adjective.
2. Do not pluralize the trademark or use it as a possessive.
3. Always use the trademark with a generic term.
4. Indicate the trademark clearly in print.
5. Use the word 'registered', the symbol ® or ™.

Policing Trademarks

Observing correct trademark usage will ensure that, if challenged, your legal rights of ownership are enforceable. But a further, more severe threat can exist if third parties infringe your rights through unauthorized use of your mark. Such infringement can severely narrow, if not eliminate the scope of protection to which the trademark is entitled or, worse, render the mark abandoned. For example the makers of Mr Muscle kitchen cleaner should be careful that others do not use the identical mark Mr Muscle on disinfectant, a seemingly related product, or use the similar name Muscleman on kitchen cleaner – each of which could weaken the trademark owner's rights in the Mr Muscle mark.

It is now widely acknowledged that a trademark can become an extremely valuable strategic and financial asset. The Persil trademark for detergents has been extended to Persil washing-up liquid and could well be used in other areas where its reputation for cleaning efficiency might prove useful. It is important, therefore, that potential avenues of expansion are not blocked.

In order to prevent the misuse and abuse of a company's trademark it is important that all concerned – particularly the salesforce, who are in the frontline of a company and act very much as its eyes and ears – are vigilant. The company should look out for any use or abuse by those dealing with the company, for example licensees, retailers, suppliers and distributors. They should report any instances spotted to the company's trademark advisers, who should then act immediately to enforce the company's rights.

It is important too that records should be kept which show at any given time the total sales of products bearing the company's trademark. This is because the company may be required to prove that the trademark has been used on a continuing basis, for however many years and in whatever countries, if it becomes involved in registration procedures, opposition or litigation.

Many companies feature the relevant trademark on sales invoices and keep an ongoing record of all invoices sent to customers. This information, together with copies of advertisements, promotional items, product literature, packaging materials, price lists and so on relating to the product bearing the trademark, can be of considerable assistance in the maintenance of international trademark rights.

Policing Trademarks

A company's trademarks are enduring and valuable assets; observing correct usage will help reinforce your legal rights of ownership; *however*:

- Be vigilant – other parties may infringe your rights through unauthorized use.
- If unpunished, such use may weaken your rights.
- All concerned in handling and managing the trademark should be alert to – and immediately act upon – any suspected infringement.
- To help support any action that might ensue, records should be kept of trademark use.

Litigation

In many instances it is possible to discourage the unauthorized use of your trademark by a sharp letter to the offending party. Such a letter, which should come from your in-house or external legal advisers, should draw to the attention of the offending party your registration (and thus your statutory rights in the trademark), the period you have been using your trademark (and thus your rights under 'common law', which is particularly important if the trademark is unregistered) and the nature of the goods or services for which the trademark has been used. The letter should leave the offending party in no doubt that you value your trademark and will take prompt steps to defend your rights should he or she not immediately 'cease and desist'.

In the event that this tactic fails, then you must enter into litigation to protect your rights. Before doing so, however, it is important to remember that litigation in all jurisdictions – particularly the USA – is expensive and time consuming, but sometimes it cannot be avoided. It is also important to remember that the burden of enforcing trademark rights is always on the original owner whether or not the trademark is registered. There is no miraculous judicial authority that watches over and springs to the defence of the aggrieved trademark owner, no mechanism that monitors and reacts to the unauthorized use by a third party of an identical or similar mark. It is the trademark owner's responsibility actively to protect the rights that have been conferred upon him or her by the state or have been accumulated under common law. In doing so, there are two kinds of action which can be started in jurisdictions throughout the world, those based on a registration and those based on common law rights. The first of these are generally referred to as 'infringement' actions, the others as 'passing off' (in the UK and in other jurisdictions modelled on UK law) and, elsewhere, 'unfair competition' actions.

Litigation

- Always an expensive, time-consuming expedient – but unavoidable if 'gentler' measures fail.
- Remember that the burden of enforcing trademark rights is always on the original owner – irrespective of whether the mark is registered or not.
- Litigation can take the form of 'infringement' action (for registered trademarks) and 'passing off' – or 'unfair competition' – action for unregistered marks.

Infringement

The state confers very powerful rights on a trademark owner through registration – which is in effect a monopoly in the use of the trademark in relation to the goods or services of interest to the owner. In the past, statutory trademark rights under UK law were confined to the precise goods or services which were covered by the registration. For example, if the Fanta trademark was registered for 'non-alcoholic drinks' in the UK the owner of that mark could not sue a third party for infringement if that third party used the Fanta mark on a can of beer or in relation to ice cream. Its rights would be limited to the common law action of 'passing off'. Following the passage of the new United Kingdom Trade Marks Act 1994, however, the provisions for infringement are now broader and would enable the owner of the Fanta trademark to sue a third party in the event that it used:

- An identical mark on identical goods or services.
- An identical mark on similar goods or a similar mark on identical or similar goods where, as a result, there is a likelihood of public confusion or association with the trademark.
- An identical or similar mark on non-similar goods if the mark has a reputation in the UK and use, without due cause, would take unfair advantage of or be detrimental to the distinctive character or reputation of the mark.

Complicated? You bet. Everyone waits to see how these provisions will be interpreted by the courts.

In the USA and other countries, the test as to whether a third party's use of the trademark in question is infringement is generally whether the usage is likely to lead to confusion, mistake or deception. Thus, if a mark is registered in the USA for a 'shampoo' and a third party uses a very similar mark on a hand cream, an eye shadow or a deodorant, such usage would be held to constitute infringement if the trademark owner can prove that there is actual confusion or a likelihood arising in the marketplace.

Infringement

- Action in law designed to enforce rights of ownership in registered trademarks.
- In the UK infringement occurs if the following are used by a third party:
  - an identical mark on identical goods or services
  - an identical mark on similar goods or services (if confusion is likely to arise)
  - a similar mark on identical or similar goods (again if confusion could arise)
  - an identical or similar mark on non-similar goods (if the infringed mark has a reputation that may be damaged).
- In the USA and other countries, the test is whether the use elsewhere of the same or similar mark is likely to cause confusion, mistake or deception.

■ 'Unfair Competition' and 'Passing Off'

While, conceptually, there are similarities between the law of 'passing off' as it exists in UK based legal systems and the law of 'unfair competition' as it applies in the USA and elsewhere, there are some important differences. 'Unfair competition' tends to acknowledge in a more eclectic way the concept of 'unfairness', while the UK courts appear more concerned with the result of the actions complained of in terms of direct financial damage rather than with the intent of or the benefit to the defendant. Under 'unfair competition' law in the United States, for example, the owner of a famous name like Rolls-Royce or Hoover would probably succeed in preventing an unauthorized third party from using its name (or similar) even in relation to totally unrelated goods or services. This would be because the defendant's actions are clearly calculated to benefit unfairly from the trademark owner's goodwill and reputation and that such goodwill and reputation might in the long term be damaged in some unquantifiable way. In the UK, the outcome of any such action based on the law of 'passing off' might very well be different.

'Passing off' and 'unfair competition' actions are usually initiated under circumstances where:

1. the plaintiff's trademark is not registered;
2. it is registered but does not cover the defendant's goods;
3. the defendant's trade dress (that is, get-up) is very similar to that used by the plaintiff but has not been registered
4. the defendant's actions generally are calculated to benefit unfairly from the plaintiff's goodwill and reputation.

However it is common to sue simultaneously for trademark infringement and 'passing off', where appropriate. If a trademark owner is to succeed in such actions, he or she must prove three things:

1. that he or she has established a reputation ('goodwill') in the trademark or trade dress in question;
2. that the use by the defendant of the similar mark or trade dress has caused, or is likely to cause, confusion in the marketplace;
3. that the trademark owner has suffered, or is likely to suffer damage as a result of the defendant's activity.

If the trademark owner can prove these three things, he or she will succeed in his suit. However, in view of the often amorphous nature of such proceedings, defendants should prosecute 'passing off' and 'unfair competition' with nothing short of utter determination and a limitless budget!

'Passing Off' and 'Unfair Competition'

- These are similar concepts in law – although 'unfair competition' (applicable in the USA and elsewhere) has a more eclectic scope.
- UK courts are more concerned with the financial damage that can arise from 'passing off'.
- To succeed with such actions a plaintiff must prove:
  - reputation in the trademark in question
  - that confusion could arise through the actions of a third party
  - that he has suffered, or is likely to suffer damage through such actions.
- Further, vital, requirements for success include an iron will and a bottomless pocket!

Remedies

If the trademark owner's suit is successful, he or she will, in most jurisdictions, be granted an injunction or an order restraining the defendant from using the mark in question. The trademark owner may also be granted an order for the delivery up for destruction of any infringing goods, descriptive labels, advertising materials, and so on, or for the erasure of the mark on any infringing goods in the possession or under the control of the defendant, as well as any deceptive labels, advertising materials and so on.

Finally, the trademark owner may obtain an order for an inquiry as to damages in respect of past interference with his rights by the defendant, or for an account of the profits made by the defendant from the sale of the infringing goods.

Many judicial systems have provision for temporary injunctions, which if granted immediately restrain a defendant's commercial activity until such time as a full hearing of the action can be undertaken. Often, but not always, the interim hearing will end the dispute – particularly if the trademark owner works quickly to assemble persuasive evidence that his business will be irreparably damaged if the defendant is allowed to pursue his activity. Normally, under such circumstances, the infringer, having been restrained, will simply abandon the project, or settle in a manner satisfactory to the trademark owners, rather than continue to a full hearing with all the cost and risk that might entail.

The Trademarks Manual

As we have discussed, trademarks can represent assets of considerable strategic and financial value to a business. Frequently trademarks are recognized internationally – thus enhancing their potency – and while provision exists within the law of almost every country of the world for the protection of the trademark owner's interests, the situation can be very complex.

In addition to the trademark owner a large number of suppliers – advertising agencies, recruitment consultants, graphic designers, printers and so on – will in the course of their business encounter and use the company's trademarks.

It is vital, therefore, that companies lay down clear rules and guidelines for the proper use and maintenance of their trademarks. Not only will this help ensure that the company's brand and corporate identities are projected in an attractive and consistent way but, critically, it will help protect their trademarks from imitators and ensure that they are not misused. These rules and guidelines ideally should cover such issues as the:

- Trademark presentation.
- The relationship between the company's corporate name and its trademarks (for example, Ford Mondeo).
- Use of any other distinguishing device (e.g. the ICI roundel).
- Use of trademarks in promotional material.
- Use of trademarks by third parties.

Graphic depictions of the company's trademarks in use should be provided and an employee of suitable seniority appointed, to ensure that the company's guidelines are adhered to on all occasions. This individual (or department) should act as 'corporate policeman' overseeing the use of the company's trademarks because only by strict compliance with the rules will they remain strong and protectable.

The Trademarks Manual

- Consistent and appropriate use of a company's trademarks is vital for 'identity management' and sustained legal protection.
- Rules and guidelines for correct trademark use must be drawn up and disseminated to all 'interested parties'.
- Critically these rules and guidelines must be enforced!

Counterfeiting

Counterfeiting is a growth industry and poses very serious problems to manufacturers of branded products; furthermore, not only can it dupe the unwitting consumer but it can cause great inconvenience to, and sometimes threaten the well-being of, those caught in its web of deception.

'Counterfeiting' is where copies, usually inferior, are represented as being merchandise of the original producer with the deliberate intent to deceive consumers and 'steal' business from the producer. It is similar to 'passing off' and 'unfair competition' and counterfeit goods can fall within both definitions.

The products which suffer most from counterfeiting tend to be those which have a high added value as a result of the 'intellectual property' inherent in the product. Thus when counterfeiting occurs it often involves infringement of a manufacturer's copyright, patent or design as well as the trademark. Engineering and pharmaceutical products are common targets for counterfeiters (with consequent risk to life and limb), as are such high margin, high profile products as fragrances, watches, luggage, videos, spirits and champagnes.

In the UK, the huge popularity of 'car boot sales' has provided a fresh conduit for counterfeit goods. Here professional traders ('spivs') jostle for space with genuine amateurs keen to raise a few pounds by selling off the unwanted contents of their attics. But the spivs have less authentic wares for sale and the public, who usually are quite aware of the conterfeit involved but regard the whole thing as 'a bit of fun', willingly enter into it. For the manufacturers whose rights are infringed it is anything but fun, and the value of counterfeit goods traded in the UK in 1994 was estimated to be £1bn.

In order to beat the counterfeiter, brand owners need to be vigilant and aggressive in protecting their intellectual property rights. In the UK counterfeiting is now a criminal offence as a result of the Copyright, Designs and Patents Act, 1988 and the US government, through GATT (General Agreement on Tariffs and Trade) negotiations, has encouraged all its trading partners to take a much tougher line on counterfeiting.

Counterfeiting

The nefarious but lucrative business of pirating or counterfeiting genuine trademark goods has too long flourished unchecked to the incalculable injury of every consumer, of every honest merchant, manufacturer and trader, and has extensively multiplied costly and tedious legislation. (Petition to US Congress in 1876)

■ 'Grey' Goods and 'Parallel Trading'

Under the Treaty of Rome, the free movement of goods within the European Union is encouraged; however, pricing structures can vary so much between countries (due, for example, to variable exchange rates) that it can be economically viable to purchase in one country, sell in another, and still undercut the manufacturer's official agent or subsidiary. In such circumstances – where manufacturers are unable adequately to control their distribution arrangements – a perfect 'grey' market is created.

The movement of goods in this way is entirely legal and is known as 'parallel trading'. But this causes profound problems for manufacturers of branded goods – irrespective of product – because the disequilibrium in prices thus created can destabilize their market positions.

The major pharmaceutical manufacturers – particularly those operating throughout Europe – tend to be particularly vulnerable. Due to varying degrees of government intervention and price subsidy, the cost to patients of prescribed medicines on a country-by-country basis differs markedly across Europe. The availability of the same drug under the same brand name with more or less the same packaging in Spain (a very low cost country) as The Netherlands (a high cost country) therefore creates a wonderful opportunity for 'freebooters' who can gain access to such products in drugs wholesalers. And even the drug companies themselves have had to keep a close eye on errant subsidiaries keen to achieve their national sales targets!

Critically, however, counterfeiters thrive in conditions where sufficient price elasticities exist to allow them plausibly to pass off their copies of genuine goods as the real thing; this is the real – and pernicious – consequence of grey markets.

'Grey' Goods and 'Parallel Trading'

- In 'common markets' like the European Union the free movement of goods is encouraged.
- Due to variations in exchange rates, price controls and other non-equivalent conditions pricing structures can vary between countries.
- This creates 'grey' market conditions and the ensuing trade that takes place – entirely legally – is known as 'parallel' trade. The pharmaceuticals industry is particularly vulnerable.
- Critically, however, counterfeiters thrive in conditions where sufficient price uncertainties exist for them to pass off their copies as the real thing.

Comparative Advertising

In the USA, it is estimated that about 30 per cent of the advertisements shown each year on network television are comparative and most of these are direct comparisons. For example, in a recent advertisement for Pepsi an unnamed cola drink is passed to the popular singer M. C. Hammer; this results in him lapsing into an uncharacteristically syrupy rendition of his hit song 'Feelings'. Only when he is supplied with Pepsi does Mr Hammer revert to his earthy street rapping tones. The voice-over identifies the unnamed drink as Coca-Cola.

In the USA, this sort of directly comparative advertising creates no legal problems whatsoever; but when the same commercial was broadcast in Japan the Japanese Fair Trade Commission forced Pepsi to take the advert off the air as comparative advertising was then (1993) barred. In the UK, they did not even try to refer to Coca-Cola because to do so would then have constituted trademark infringement.

Since the United Kingdom Trade Marks Act 1994, comparative advertising is permissible as The Act no longer prevents the use of a registered trademark by anyone to identify goods or services as those of the owner (or licensee) provided that:

- It is in accordance with honest practices in industrial and commercial matters.
- It does not, without due cause, take unfair advantage of, or is detrimental to the distinctive character or repute of the trademark.

Within this somewhat opaque wording, there are three key phrases:

- Honest practices in industrial and commercial matters
- Taking unfair advantage of the distinctive character or repute of the trademark
- Detrimental to the distinctive character or repute of the trademark

How will these legal principles be tested? In the 1996 case of *Barclays Bank plc* v *RBS Advanta*, the plaintiffs (registered proprietors of Barclaycard) failed to prevent the defendant's use of literature in which comparisons were made with their new Advanta credit card but which failed to refer to additional benefits of the plaintiff's card.

Honest Practice

A few years ago a television advertisement for Toyota carried the punch line 'The car in front is a Toyota'. Their rivals Nissan immediately responded with a press advert saying 'The car in front of the Toyota is a Nissan Primera'. It is accepted practice in the UK motor trade that there should be comparative advertising and all parties take a reasonably relaxed view; a measure of self-restraint is sensibly applied. As the change in the law is very new, it will be interesting to see whether the current practice, when tested, is deemed 'honest' and allowed to continue.

■ Unfair Advantage

In the USA, a perfume was recently advertised as smelling very similar to the well-known Giorgio perfume; it featured the Giorgio bottle alongside the 'smellalike' to reinforce the point. In the UK this would now probably be deemed to take unfair advantage of the distinctive character or repute of the Giorgio mark.

■ Detrimental to Character or Repute

In a case in 1993 under the old law, the court stopped the L'Arôme's 'smellalike' perfumes which were displayed alongside those of Chanel in L'Arôme's 'consultants manual'. Under the new law the case would probably be decided in the same way and would be regarded as causing detriment to the distinctive character or repute of the Chanel mark – particularly as the smellalikes often do not have the same quality of ingredients.

The law relating to comparative advertising in the UK is new and open to further interpretation by the courts. It has widely been criticized as too general and not specific enough for a UK statute – which is exasperating for trademark owners, but probably very good news for lawyers!

Comparative Advertising

- Comparative advertising – often involving explicit use of a competitor's trademark – is common practice in the USA.
- In the UK, the motor trade, computer manufacturers and airlines have all been involved in comparative advertising but their activities, to an extent, have been self-regulated.
- The new Trade Marks Act now permits the use of a registered trademark by anyone in advertising:
  - provided it is in accordance with *honest practices* in industrial and commercial matters; and
  - that it does not, without due cause, take *unfair advantage* of or is not *detrimental to the distinctive character or repute* of the trademark.
- Clearly these provisions will be wide open to debate!

CHAPTER 5

Managing and Exploiting Brands

Maintaining Brand Equities

If a brand is to be exploited successfully by the trademark owner – or, more distantly, through licensees – it must possess distinctive appeals that invest it with commercial attractiveness. These appeals, referred to frequently as 'equities', are embodied in the physical or emotional satisfactions that the product or service delivers and are symbolized by the brand name and get up. The brand thus guarantees the authenticity of the product or service and thereby assures the purchaser that his requirements will be met.

In maintaining brand equities, the owner must ensure that the product or service concerned is fulfilling its basic 'promise' – be this sustenance, refreshment, cleaning power, relief from pain, peace of mind, amusement or whatever. Next, the owner must ensure that the brand's promise is relevant to contemporary requirements, and adapt the product or service accordingly. Then he or she must ensure that the visual presentation of the brand – trademarks, pack graphics and so on – is clear, consistent and distinctive, so that the brand remains instantly recognizable, no matter how cluttered the marketplace.

Finally, the brand owner must ensure that the brand's promise is communicated to its market in an attractive and appealing way. Again, consistency is the key and advertising should be used to promote the product or service so that the brand's personality – its 'tone of voice' – remains unchanged over time.

Consistency is the hallmark of great brands. Brands like Kodak, Coca-Cola, Kellogg's, American Express and Mercedes have all remained true to their promise over the years – but all have adapted to the changing needs of the consumer. Constant attention to – and investment in – the brand's substantive and visual equities is therefore required to ensure that the brand continues to meet the requirements of the marketplace. It is worth remembering that brands exist only with the consent of the consumer; if they fail to deliver then this consent will be withdrawn.

Maintaining Brand Equities

- A brand's 'equities' are its distinctive appeals, as perceived by the consumer.
- These are embodied in the physical or emotional satisfactions that the product or service delivers and are symbolized by the trademark which guarantees that the brand will remain true to its promise.
- The brand owner must constantly attend to – and invest in – his brand's equities; failure to do so may result in loss of sales – or even the demise of the brand.

The Role of Design

Those companies whose trademarks and logos are applied coherently and consistently benefit because the image they project to the world is one of coherence and consistency – customers, suppliers and others perceive the company as 'having its act together', as knowing what it is doing, of being well organized and of being efficient. Conversely, a muddled, inconsistent projection of a company's trademarks and logos will damage the company's image.

It is clear, however, that a company needs to project more than just a coherent image and message; these need to be contemporary and relevant. For this reason advertising needs to be up-dated from time to time, as does packaging, the products themselves, the methods of production and so on.

This is also true of logos and trademarks. They too need to be reviewed from time to time and updated, otherwise they will become hopelessly old-fashioned. The dilemma for companies, however, is that it requires a great deal of time and, normally, a great deal of investment for logos and trademarks to acquire a familiarity and potency in the marketplace. It has been noted that advertisements and jingles often start to make an impact with consumers just when the advertiser and the advertising agency are beginning to get heartily sick of them. Of course, the consumer is exposed to them on far fewer occasions than the company or the agency and is also less interested in them.

So it takes a lot of time and effort to establish trademarks and logos in the public consciousness. It is, therefore, important to be careful, even reluctant, when changing them. Certainly, change for change's sake, because the company has become bored with the old logo or because a new person on the scene wants to implant his or her own personality, is to be avoided.

But trademarks and logos do become outmoded and old-fashioned, and they do need to be overhauled and kept up to date. Normally the overhaul should consist of an updating of the design while the key visual elements are retained. Ideally, there should be a strong continuity in the design, and the loyalties and values inherent in the old trademark and logo should be carried over to the new design without a hitch. Research is therefore required in order to establish what, in the eyes of consumers of the brand, are the key visual equities.

The symbols and logos of Shell, BP, Coca-Cola, Kodak, Volkswagen, IBM, Mercedes, Prudential Insurance and scores of other major corporations have been updated innumerable times without in any way diluting the equity already invested in these logos. BP is an excellent example of a company which has been through a major 'corporate identity' change. This involved only a minor modification to the BP logo (Image 26) but the wholesale application of the colour green to garage forecourts, and so on. The overall effect has been a dramatic re-imaging of the BP brand and BP, interestingly, has succeeded in registering the colour green as one of its trademarks in a number of countries.

Smaller corporations should in most cases adopt the same policy – even to the point of re-introducing equities which over time may have fallen into disuse. Red Funnel Ferries was founded in 1861 to provide the first regular ferry service between Southampton and the Isle of Wight. The company registered its red funnel with the single black band as a trademark, but with the passing of the age of steam, funnels became obsolete. Red Funnel's latest identity re-introduces in a modern and appealing way this traditional equity (Image 27).

Relationship with Advertising Agencies and Other Advisers

Few trademark owners nowadays have the resources – or the desire – to produce and place their own advertising, handle the development of packaging design, mount a public relations campaign or conduct a consumer research survey. Instead they employ external advisers to assist them.

Yet as these activities are so closely connected with the maintenance of brand equities, is the trademark owner, by delegating responsibility for these tasks to third parties, not guilty of negligence? If the advisers concerned are not as intimately aware as the trademark owner of the 'essence' of the brand, then the answer is yes. Most owners therefore make it their business to ensure that their advisers are very fully briefed on the history of the brand and the current and future role it is expected to play in the organization.

It is perhaps no coincidence that some of the world's most successful brands enjoy relationships with their advisers that go back over very many years. The advertising agency BBDO has held the Wrigley's Chewing Gum account since 1933 and DDB Needham has handled Pepsi Cola's advertising since 1960. Similarly, in the United Kingdom, SH Benson was responsible for the famous Guinness advertising for over 40 years until it lost the account to J Walter

Thompson in the late 1960s. The account later moved to Ogilvy & Mather (which a few years ago absorbed the old SH Benson agency).

In order to get the best and most valuable work out of such important – and expensive – advisers as advertising agencies, design companies and PR consultants, it is vital that all involved not only understand and respect the equities of the brand concerned but realize that they are, essentially, servants of the brand. In this role they are to a limited extent guardians of the brand's equity. Ultimately, however, it is the trademark owner and the owner's management teams who are responsible for protecting and nurturing the brand and they who are answerable to shareholders and investors for managing the brand for profit and growth.

Relationship with Advisers

- Advertising agencies, design companies, public relations consultants, market researchers, and so on all play a vital role in helping to build and maintain brand equities.
- To contribute fully to this process, it is critically important that such advisers are intimately aware of the essence of the brand and its strategic role within the trademark owner's organization.
- Such advisers, however, are essentially servants of the brand. Ultimate responsibility for protecting and nurturing the brand belongs to the trademark owner. It is the trademark owner who must manage the asset for profit and growth.

Brand Extension

Much has been written in recent years about brand extension as a means of introducing new products to the marketplace without the high cost and risk involved in developing and launching new brands. Brand extension offers the brand owner the possibility of endowing a new product with some or all of the qualities of an existing brand. The company can thus utilize the reputation of the existing brand to enter a market more cheaply, establish the new product more quickly and increase the overall exposure of the brand. Mars Ice Cream is a brilliantly successful example. The company has clearly captured within the new product all the key qualities of the Mars Bar – thick chocolate, a delicious chewy centre and a thoroughly self-indulgent treat!

This strategy, safe though it may appear, is not without cost and risk: by extending the brand to cover a new product brand owners face the possibility that all they are doing is diluting the appeal of their existing brand. How?

- *By extending the brand to embrace products which are dissonant with the values of the existing brand* Cadbury, somewhat disastrously, extended its famous brand in the 1960s to embrace instant mashed potato; the strategy succeeded in obtaining widespread acceptance for the new product but over time damaged Cadbury's unique reputation in chocolate confectionery. More recently Ranks Hovis McDougall, which for many years had successfully built the Hovis brand of brown wholemeal bread, with the addition of fibre-rich country grain, granary and similar varieties, has introduced Hovis *white* bread. This is positioned in the premium sector, which is eating away that of the standard loaf and it will be interesting to see if the power of the Hovis name as a symbol of 'traditional goodness' can sustain the brand's credibility in this new area.
- *By extending the brand to embrace products of inferior quality to the existing brand* Widespread dissemination of the Pierre Cardin brand to articles as commonplace as silk ties, and as bizarre as Japanese 'toilet slippers', has cheapened a once-fine brand name. Equally, one cannot escape the conclusion that it was the availability of original food technology that encouraged Kellogg's to 'force fit' the unhappy Pop Tarts product into their breakfast foods portfolio.
- *By sequestering loyal consumers of a property they may have felt to be exclusively theirs and, without their advice or consent, exploiting this in a way that outrages and marginalizes them* Both Mercedes and BMW attracted considerable criticism some years ago when they introduced smaller and cheaper versions of their distinguished limousines. Similarly Volkswagen may be alienating loyal VW customers by co-branding Seat and Skoda in advertising.

On the other hand, brand extension (of both 'product brands' and 'house brands') has proved in many cases to be a remarkably successful strategy. It has reduced the cost and risk of new product launches, increased the exposure of brands, made brands more attractive and contemporary to consumers and, in many instances, has extended the brand's life. Small wonder then that during the recent recession, which has affected most Western economies, brand extension has been a popular – if perhaps over-used – strategy. It is apparent therefore that brand extension is entirely practical – but it is equally apparent that it needs to be treated with considerable care and skill.

Brand Extension

- Brand extension is a popular, less risky way of successfully introducing new products (and services).
- It is done by identifying the key attributes of the brand (these may be emotional, and/or physical) and using these as the basis for developing new products.
- Mars Ice Cream has become highly successful because the product is faithful to the Mars Bar 'promise' and delivers very similar satisfactions.
- Equally, Barclaycall's direct banking service has attracted a strong following because customers have responded positively to the 'trustworthiness' of the Barclays name.
- A successful brand extension will always have the effect of strengthening the 'parent' brand.

■ The Internationalisation of Trademarks

The possibility of developing new international brands rather than simply national brands is a highly attractive one to brand owners. International brands exercise potent appeals with consumers, give brand owners substantial economies in such areas as production, inventory, advertising and promotion and provide companies with a powerful unity in their international activities.

Over the last few years, a multitude of factors has combined to help create conditions which favour international brands. These include vastly improved communications, increased travel, better language tuition in schools, the creation of free trade areas like the European Union and the European Free Trade Area, the 'opening up' of eastern Europe, and dramatic economic growth in the Far East. The world has indeed become a smaller place and international markets for standardized consumer products are rapidly opening up.

How then can companies develop their brands to take advantage of the international market opportunities that are becoming available? There are a series of strategic and practical considerations to be borne in mind.

■ Strategic Considerations

A characteristic that is shared by all truly international brands is their *coherence*. Coca-Cola looks and tastes the same just about everywhere; so do

Mars Bars, Heineken beer and Marlboro cigarettes. It follows then that in order to join this exclusive club, aspiring international brands must have core appeals that are reproduceable on a country-by-country basis.

Practical Considerations

Although coherence is the basic strategic requirement for developing international brands, there must of course be 'freedom within the law'. The way in which the product is used and the satisfactions which it delivers must remain the same; but the product itself, the positioning, the packaging, the advertising and, to a very limited extent, the branding can all be modified to suit 'local' market conditions.

Some years ago the makers of Brylcreem, intrigued why their popular hair cream was selling so well in West Africa, decided to carry out some consumer research. This established that Brylcreem was being purchased in large quantities by housewives and used as an exotic form of cooking fat! It is doubtful therefore whether Brylcreem, on this evidence, qualifies as a truly international brand.

Contrast this with Oil of Ulay. Unilever markets this brand under the Oil of Ulay name in the United Kingdom, but the brand carries different but related brand names in other countries, for example Oil of Olay and Oil of Olaz. Despite these differences, the product, the label, the packaging and the advertising message are all basically the same, and the brand is seen quite clearly as an integrated international proposition.

However, if a new brand, in the course of its development, is considered to have international potential, it is essential at the outset to establish a brand name which is suitable for use and protectable on an international basis. It is the name more than any other element of the marketing 'mix' that most completely encapsulates the appeals of the product and acts as a focal point for promotional investment. Thus as the trend towards the international branding of goods and services continues to strengthen, companies must increasingly adopt strategies to ensure that the brand names they use are the same in all markets.

Successful International Branding

Simply put, the features that make up a successful international brand are as follows.

- *At the core of the brand must lie strong intellectual property rights to which the brand's owner has clear legal title.* Registered trademarks protecting the brand name itself are usually the key property rights in a brand but design rights, copyrights and patents may also contribute powerfully. (Kodak, for example, is a trademark of Eastman Kodak Company, which is registered on an international basis; the machines or the processes used to manufacture Kodak products may be protected by patent; the artwork on the packaging may be protected by copyright; the shape of the container or general appearance of the product may be protected by design.) In the absence of intellectual property rights, brands cannot exist – they will merely be undifferentiated generics.

- *The brand must be powerfully and meaningfully differentiated* It must stand apart from its competitors such that consumers recognize that the branded product has particular characteristics, both tangible and intangible. Unless brands are differentiated, no brand personality exists and the consumer has no reason to select any one brand in preference to another.
- *The brand must be appealing* The consumer must recognize, in the brand, qualities and attributes which are desirable and which prompt recommendation and repurchase.
- *The brand must be consistent* It must continue to deliver satisfactions and must not let the consumer down.
- *The brand must be supported through advertising and other forms of promotion and through distribution* The consumer must be aware of the brand and its qualities and it must, too, be available for the consumer to purchase.
- *The brand must address consumer needs which exist internationally* No brand can become international if the satisfactions it delivers are purely local in nature.
- *Most importantly, the brand must be meticulously managed over an extended period of time* Quality must be maintained, distribution ensured and competitive challenges met. And, as mentioned above, appropriate and appealing advertising is required, modified to suit changing needs and conditions and consistent and appealing packaging must be used to help existing purchasers recognize the product as well as to attract new purchasers to it. Brand extension may also be required to exploit the 'equity' in the brand to keep the brand relevant and appealing, but this too needs careful and skilful management.

What distinguishes the world's leading brands, both international and national, is the care and attention which are lavished on them by their owners. Good brand management requires singlemindedness, a streak of fanaticism and an attention to detail which sets it apart from the normal.

The top 20 brands across Europe and in five top European markets are shown in Tables 5.1 and 5.2. The following 14 countries have been included in the analysis: Austria, Belgium, Denmark, Finland, France, Germany, Great Britain, Ireland, Italy, The Netherlands, Norway, Portugal, Spain, Switzerland.

Successful International Branding

- At the core of the brand must reside rock-solid intellectual property rights.
- The brand must be powerfully and meaningfully differentiated.
- The brand must appeal.
- The brand must be consistent.
- The brand must be supported.
- The brand must address universal needs and wants.
- The brand must be *meticulously managed.*

Table 5.1 The Top 20 European Brands, 1996

Brand		*Sales ($ m.)*
1	Coca-Cola	3590
2	Ariel	1450
3	Pampers	1360
4	Barilla Pasta	1105
5	Jacobs coffee	1070
6	Nescafé	940
7	Danone yoghurt	820
8	Whiskas	790
9	Parmigiano–Reggiano parmesan	735
10	Pedigree	590
11	Langnese ice cream	570
12	Persil detergents	555
13	Fanta	550
14	Pepsi Cola	525
15	Milka	505
16	Dash	485
17	Danone fromage frais	480
18	Grana Padano parmesan	455
19=	Scottex toilet paper	445
19=	Danone chilled desserts	445

Source: Checkout/Nielsen.

Table 5.2 The Top Fives, 1994

	Brand	*Sales ($m.)*
	All soft drinks	
1	Coca-Cola	3590
2	Fanta	550
3	Pepsi	525
4	Sprite	280
5	Evian	260
	All detergents	
1	Ariel	1450
2	Persil (Henkel)	555
3	Dash	485
4	Skip	420
5	Persil (Unilever)	385
	All coffee	
1	Jacobs	1070
2	Nescafé	940
3	Lavazza	405
4	Douwe Egberts	395
5	Tchibo	370
	All petfood	
1	Whiskas	790
2	Pedigree	590
3	KiteKat	345
4	Sheba	225
5	Friskies	205
	All yoghurts	
1	Danone	820
2	Yoplait	340
3	Chambourcy	315
4	Müller	285
5	Yomo	220

Source: Checkout/Nielsen.

Trademark Licensing

Trademark licensing, in general, is the practice of allowing others to use your trademarks on approved goods or services under terms which allow you to control the quality of the goods or services covered by the licence. In its most common form, trademark licensing is the licensing of third parties to produce or offer to supply more or less the same goods or services as those produced by the trademark owner. In the United Kingdom, for example, Whitbread holds the licence to brew and distribute Heineken beer, an activity that is wholly complementary to its main business. Heineken rigorously monitors and controls the quality of the Heineken beer that Whitbread produces under the terms of the licence and ensures that the marketing of the brand is carried out in a way that is generally supportive of its international 'positioning' objectives.

The licensing of technological know-how and patents has long been established and it is accepted that often significant royalties should be paid by licensees for their use. Moreover, the agreements governing such licences are often very complex and recognize that the maintenance of the value of the intangible asset is an important task and is the duty of both the licensor and the licensee. Until recently, however, trademark licences were not treated as seriously and indeed sometimes were just added in as the 'icing on the cake' of patent/technology licences. But the increasing awareness of the value of brands has prompted brand owners to wake up to the notion that, although intangible, such properties *do* have significant value and that their licensing cannot be regarded as a mere formality.

One of the first effects of this is that licence agreements with third parties now more clearly acknowledge the fact that the property being licensed is valuable. Higher royalty rates are being demanded (and justified) and stricter conditions to ensure the proper use and maintenance of trademarks – both in legal terms and in marketing terms – are put in place. For example, it is not uncommon to find third-party licensees (and not just of luxury goods brands) being subjected to the strictest quality inspections. Their duty as licensees is more onerous but at the same time their contribution is seen as greater. For example, licensees will often now participate with the brand owner in the development of global advertising campaigns and the design of visual identity programmes. It is only in this way that the integrity, and thus the value, of a brand can be safeguarded.

Needless to say, it is crucial to find the right partner. As with any form of brand extension activity the net result should not merely be enhanced short-term revenues but a fundamental strengthening of the parent brand. Rolls-Royce pursues a licensing policy which is designed to maintain the exclusivity of the brand rather than generate additional income. It does this by appointing licences in certain of the many product sectors where its famous name, logo, 'Spirit of Ecstasy' badge, etc. are habitually 'ripped off' by unauthorized users. These licensees are chosen on the basis of the quality and exclusivity of the products they manufacture, and, in addition to providing appropriate 'company' for the brand, act as a highly motivated monitoring system which locates infringements at an early stage and allows Rolls-Royce to deal with them before they have developed too far.

Coca-Cola too has a licensing policy but the financial benefits it derives from this are probably far more significant than those of Rolls-Royce. Coca-Cola licensed Murjani (agreement terminated some years ago), an American-based clothing company well known for its success with the Gloria Vanderbilt range of jeans, to produce a range of Coca-Cola branded sportswear. Millions of consumers responded to this and, in doing so, turned themselves into walking billboards, to the greater benefit of the famous Coca-Cola name and logo.

Licensing

- In its most common form, licensing is the granting of a right to use the trademark concerned in relation to very similar goods or services.
- However, the trademark owner must ensure that he exercises absolute control over the quality of the goods and services produced by the licensee, and marketed under its trademark.
- Licensing can be a highly lucrative and relatively risk-free way of exploiting the brand.
- It can also provide strategic benefits to the trademark owner in broadening the brand's exposure and enhancing its image.

Internal Trademark Licensing

Trademark licences are not only used with third parties. Many companies (of which Nestlé is a notable example) have a policy of owning all intellectual property centrally and charging subsidiaries for its use. Thus, for example, even though many of the brands acquired as part of the Rowntree takeover a few years ago are purely British (Quality Street, After Eight, and so on), they are all now owned by the Swiss company and licensed back to the English company. International trademark licensing has a number of implications:

- Internal licences, whether within the home country or overseas, increasingly incorporate the payment of a royalty which reflects the true value of the

asset being used rather than just being a nominal amount to 'cover administration'. Making a financial charge for the use of a trademark (or other intellectual property) focuses the user on the value of the asset and the need both to protect and exploit that value.
- The royalties received from licences to overseas subsidiaries can be used to repatriate funds in return for the use of a genuine piece of property. This can have major fiscal implications.
- New licences negotiated within the group and outside the group, can be placed in a context of genuine brand licensing giving the opportunity to negotiate much higher returns for the use of brands than has been the case commonly in the past.

The fiscal implication of charging overseas subsidiaries and third-party licensees a proper rental for the use of brands can be significant. Many companies, however, have yet to realize that the royalty rates they demand are far too small for the value of the trademark asset being licensed. Many companies also either fail to benefit from proper internal licensing arrangements, or risk the likelihood of problems from tax authorities from the arrangements they do have in place.

It is clear therefore that a great many trademark owners would benefit from the availability of 'international standards' for trademark licensing rather than the mish-mash that characterizes current practice – usually a trade off between what has happened in the past and what is acceptable to the tax authorities. The availability of international standards would pave the way for the development of techniques that took into account the requirements of both the trademark owner and the tax authorities. It goes without saying that such techniques should be robust and transparent and logically should commence with an independent valuation of the brand concerned. This would allow both the brand owner and the licensee to establish, from an objective auditable base, the contribution of the brand to the licensee's business and therefore the royalty that could be charged.

Franchising

The franchise industry is now a huge and mature one and is global in scope. It continues to expand and in the last twenty years or so there has been tremendous growth in the area of catering, retailing and the provision of services. McDonald's fast food restaurants, Interflora 'flower relay', Dyno-Rod drain and pipe cleaning and Prontaprint printing and copying shops are all examples of highly successful franchised businesses.

Franchising involves the granting of rights to a number of licensees in different geographical areas. Frequently the rights being licensed are not just intellectual property rights such as trademarks and logos but include access to the business system developed by the licensor. Thus franchise agreements

Internal Trademark Licensing

- Internal trademark licensing can enhance substantially the strategic and financial value of the brand to its owner.
- The process of calculating brand royalty rates, however, is something of a 'black art': no generally recognized standards and procedures exist and practice can vary widely between companies.
- Consequently many trademark owners are either failing to benefit from proper internal licensing arrangements, or risk the likelihood of problems from tax authorities with the arrangements they do have in place.
- More logical and robust licensing systems are required; such systems should be based upon the value of the brand being licensed.
- This would allow both the trademark owner and the licensee to establish, from an objective and auditable base, the contribution of the brand to the licensee's business, and therefore the royalty that could be charged.

often cover the look and design of the business, the uniforms of employees, promotional materials and so forth. In addition, the benefits provided by the franchisor frequently include staff training, specialized accountancy and business control systems, assistance with staff selection and so on.

It is very much in the interest of the franchisor to ensure that their product or service is delivered in a way that is consistent with the highest quality standards. Their trademark acts as a guarantee of this and is frequently therefore the most potent asset involved in a franchising deal. After all, once a franchise is successfully established, the franchisor can hardly take back their know-how; but if the franchisee fails to pay the licence fee, operate the franchise in the approved fashion or terminates or breaks the franchise agreement for some reason, the franchisor can and will withdraw the right to use their trademark, copyright and other intellectual property rights.

In all forms of trademark licensing and franchising it is clearly essential to ensure that the trademarks and other forms of intellectual property involved in the deal are protected by registration in the countries where rights are to be licensed. Most countries do not, in fact, recognize licensing of trademarks for goods or services unless there is a valid trademark registration, but even where they do it can be a highly risky procedure. It is also prudent to record the licensee as a registered user as this avoids the possibility of cancellation proceedings against the trademark owner on the grounds of non-use; it also makes the licence a matter of public record.

Franchising

- Franchising is the granting of intellectual property rights to a number of licensees in different geographical areas.
- It frequently includes access to the business system developed by the licensor.
- McDonald's, Dyno-Rod, Interflora and Pronta-print are all examples of successful franchised businesses.

Monitoring 'Brand Value'

A brand is a name or sign – and its associated tangible and emotional attributes – which is intended to identify the goods or services of one seller in order to differentiate them from those of competitors. At the heart of a brand are trademark rights.

Because a brand designates a product or service as being different from competitors' products and services, it establishes a 'pact' between the supplier and the consumer. This pact is an on-going relationship between supplier and consumer and, because of this, brands provide a security of demand which the supplier would not otherwise enjoy. This security of demand means a security of earnings and this is what lies at the heart of brand value.

In today's competitive environment, many companies have come to recognize the value of brands. This is evidenced in a number of ways. Developing new brands is taken more seriously than ever before, the protection of brands and trademark rights has a higher profile, and old brands that seemed dormant are now being revitalized and extended.

In view of the huge cost and risk of developing new brands, many companies have improved and extended their brand portfolios through acquisition and brands now play a major role in much merger activity. The amounts paid in the late 1980s for Kraft, General Foods and RJR Nabisco in the USA, and for Rowntree in Europe demonstrated how much money people were prepared to put behind their belief in the value of brands. Indeed, even though in the USA it is not possible to do so, in some countries brands are now being put on company balance sheets as recognized intangible assets.

But the most noticeable evidence of this increased recognition of the value and importance of brands is that today brands are being discussed not just by marketers and trademark attorneys, but by accountants, bankers, taxation lawyers, investors, and corporate presidents and vice-presidents.

Two quotations illustrate this. John Stuart, former chairman of Quaker said: 'If this business were split up, I would be glad to take the brands, trademarks and goodwill and you could have all the bricks and mortar and I would fare better than you.' Per Gyllenhammar of Volvo put the same point more succinctly: 'Our most valuable asset is the Volvo trademark.'

The Concept of Brand Value

- Brands symbolize the 'pact' between the supplier and the consumer; as long as the supplier fulfills his side of the bargain then the consumer will continue to buy.
- Brands can therefore provide security of demand and this, in turn, means security of earnings; this is what lies at the heart of brand value.
- The concept of brand value is now widely understood: brands are acknowledged as economic assets of high importance and have become the subject of strategies designed to exploit their appeal and potency.
- Brands have also come to play a major role in merger and acquisition activity – firm evidence that the world of banking and finance now regards brands as legitimate vehicles for investment.

■ Brands on the Balance Sheet

The practice of brand valuation was developed because of the need to recognize brand value in balance sheets. This arose because the amount that was being paid for companies in the mid to late 1980s was becoming increasingly higher than the value of the company's net tangible assets and this was creating problems in accounting for goodwill ('goodwill' is what remains when the value of an acquired company's net tangible assets is subtracted from the price paid by the purchaser). A study of acquisitions in the 1980s showed that whereas in 1981 net tangible assets represented 82 per cent of the amount bid for companies, by 1987 this had fallen to just 30 per cent. It became clear that companies were being acquired less for their tangible assets and more for their intangible assets (see Table 5.3).

Table 5.3 The Growth of Intangible Value

	Net tangibles as % of target company's value	*Goodwill and intangibles as % of target company's value*
1981	82	18
1983	72	28
1985	34	66
1987	30	70
1990	28	72

But accounting practice for dealing with so-called goodwill did not deal with this and the result was that companies were penalised for making what they believed to be good acquisitions. They either had to suffer massive goodwill write-down charges on their profit and loss accounts, or they had to write off the entire amount against the reserves in their balance sheet and in many cases end up, illogically, with a lower level of net assets than before the acquisition.

However, in countries such as the UK, France, Sweden, Australia and New Zealand, it was possible to recognize the value of brands as 'identifiable intangible assets' and put these on the balance sheet of the acquiring company. This helped resolve the problem of goodwill. In the mid-1980s, the UK's Reckitt & Colman put on its balance sheet a value of the Airwick brand which it had recently bought; Grand Metropolitan, which had acquired the Smirnoff brand as part of Heublein did the same. At this time too some newspaper groups, notably the *Daily Telegraph* in London and Murdoch-owned News International in Australia, put the value of their acquired mastheads on their balance sheets.

In 1988, in collaboration with the London Business School, Interbrand, the international branding consultancy, conducted the first 'whole portfolio' valuation for the UK foods group, Ranks Hovis McDougall. This established that it was possible to value brands not only when they had been acquired but also when they had been created by the company themselves (after all, it did not make sense to say that the Burger King brand possessed identifiable values but the McDonald's brand did not just because it had never changed hands).

In 1989, the London Stock Exchange endorsed the concept of brand valuation as used by Ranks Hovis McDougall and there followed a wave of major branded goods companies which recognized the value of brands as intangible assets on balance sheets. In the UK these included Cadbury Schweppes, Grand Metropolitan (when they acquired Pillsbury for $5 billion), Guinness, Ladbrokes (when they acquired Hilton) and United Biscuits (including the Keebler brand). In France, brands were put on the balance sheet by, among others, Pernod Ricard, Eridiana Béghin-Say and Group Danone (who have valued brands such as Bel Paese, Volvic, Lea & Perrins and Danone). In Australia and New Zealand, balance sheet valuations have been carried out by most major branded goods companies including Pacific Dunlop, News International and Lion Nathan.

Although the number of multi-million pound acquisitions taking place has lessened somewhat in recent years, accountants are still debating the rights and wrongs of balance sheet recognition. However, it now looks increasingly likely that the UK's Accounting Standards Board will endorse the idea – for so long accepted by branded goods companies themselves – that brands are real assets and should appear on corporate balance sheets.

In the UK, USA and in other parts of the world one thing is clear: brands do comprise a significant element of business value. What is more, for many businesses, the brand element of their overall 'worth' is often more important than the tangible assets that traditionally have been regarded as representing the core value of a company.

Brands on the Balance Sheet

- Balance sheet brand valuations first arose because of the problem of accounting for goodwill on acquisitions.
- In countries such as the UK, France, Sweden, Australia and New Zealand it is possible to recognize the value of brands in the balance sheet. This helps resolve the problem of goodwill write-offs.
- Since 1988 – Ranks Hovis McDougall's historic decision to include all their brands in their balance sheet – many major companies have recognized the value of their brands in this way.

How to Value a Brand

The value of a brand, like that of any other economic asset, is the worth *now* of the benefits of future ownership. In order to calculate brand value it is necessary to identify clearly:

- The actual benefits of future ownership; that is, the current and future earnings or cash flows of the brand.
- Their security and predictability and, therefore, the multiple (of profits) or discount rate (to cash flows) which can with confidence be applied.

The valuation approach developed by Interbrand works on the premise that it is the brand's strength which determines the discount rate, or multiple, to apply to brand earnings – a strong brand provides a high level of confidence that brand earnings will be maintained and results in a low discount rate or a high multiple. Conversely, with a weak brand the level of confidence in future earnings is low, so the discount rate must be high, or the multiple low.

This system of brand valuation, focused on brand earnings and brand strength, has proved to be robust and auditable, provided always that the requisite marketing, financial and trademark legal skills are brought together.

■ Brand Earnings

A vital factor in determining the value of a brand is therefore its profitability or potential profitability over time. However, to arrive at a balance sheet value it is not enough merely to apply a simple discount rate or multiplier to post-tax profits. A brand may be essentially a commodity product or may gain much of its profitability from non-brand related factors. The elements of profitability which do not result from the brand's identity must therefore be excluded. Secondly, the valuation itself may, in the case of an earnings multiple system, be materially affected by using a single, possibly unrepresentative, year's profit. For this reason, a smoothing element should be introduced, or better still a thorough preparation of future cashflow statements. This could be the basis of a discounted cash flow model, though it must also incorporate a thorough review of expected performance.

■ Brand Strength

The determination of the discount rate or the multiple to be applied to brand earnings is derived from an in-depth assessment of brand strength. This requires a detailed review of each brand, its positioning, the market in which it operates, competition, past performance, future plans, risks to the brand and so on. The brand strength is a composite of seven weighted factors, each of which is scored according to clearly established and consistent guidelines:

1. *Market* Brands in markets such as food and drinks are intrinsically more valuable than brands in, for example, high tech, or clothing areas, as these latter markets are more vulnerable to technological or fashion changes.
2. *Stability* Long-established brands which command consumer loyalty and have become part of the 'fabric' of their markets are particularly valuable.
3. *Leadership* A brand which leads its market sector is a more stable and valuable property than a brand lower down the order or one with less influence.
4. *Trend* The overall long-term trend of the brand is an important measure of its ability to remain contemporary and relevant to consumers and hence of its value.

5. *Support* Those brand names which have received consistent investment and focused support must be regarded as more valuable than those which have not. Though the amount spent in supporting a brand is important, the quality of this support is equally significant.
6. *Internationality* Brands which are international are inherently more valuable than national or regional brands.
7. *Protection* A registered trademark is a statutory monopoly in a name or device, or in a combination of these. Other protection may exist in common law, at least in certain countries. The strength and breadth of the brand's protection is critical in assessing its worth.

The brand is scored for each of these factors according to different weightings and the resultant total, known as the 'brand strength score', is expressed as a percentage. These scores are applied in a consistent, logical and verifiable manner.

■ Attributing A Discount Rate or Multiple

The strength of a brand directly determines the reliability of future income flows from that brand so the brand strength analysis can be used to determine the discount rate or the multiple to apply to the brand-related profits. Thus the stronger the brand the lower the discount rate or the greater the multiple. The relationship between brand strength and brand value follows a normal distribution and is represented by a classic 'S' curve. The shape of the curve is influenced by the following factors:

- As a brand's strength increases from virtually zero (an unknown or new brand) to a position as number three or four in a national market, the value increases gradually.
- As a brand moves into the number two or weak number one position in its market and/or becomes known internationally there is a stronger effect on its value.
- Once a brand is established as a powerful world brand its value no longer increases at the same incremental rate even if market share internationally is improved.

In fixing the discount rate or the multiple to be applied to the brand strength score the closest available analogy to the return from a notional perfect brand is the return from a risk-free investment. However, the perfect brand does not operate in a risk-free environment. Allowances for these factors must be taken into account when determining the discount rate or the multiple to be applied for a brand operating in a real business environment. Thus the lowest discount rate or the highest multiple that can be applied will be somewhat lower than that for a risk-free investment and may vary from business to business and industry to industry.

■ Other Valuation Applications

This section has focused mainly on the technical aspects of valuation for balance sheet purposes, both of 'home grown' and acquired brands. There are, of course, many other situations where brand valuations can usefully be used and where the same basic technique can be applied. These include mergers and acquisitions, fund-raising, licensing, brand management and brand strategy development. The assessment of the strength of the brand is unlikely to change greatly whatever the situation and this is the area of the valuation process which normally requires the most detailed and time-consuming investigations. However, attributable brand earnings and the appropriate multiple could vary considerably as in the case of acquisitions. For example, synergy benefits can be identified and incorporated into the brand profits. It may also be appropriate to include an acquisition premium.

> Where a bidder has understood total asset values better than the market, a valuation of intangible assets will prevent companies being purchased too cheaply. (Warburg Securities)

CHAPTER 6

Case History: The 'Transax' Story

Background

The reluctance of the major British clearing banks to provide their customers with cheque cards guaranteeing payment of amounts *in excess* of a miserly hundred pounds has played right into the hands of the credit and charge card operators. And who benefits from a substantial share of credit and charge card transactions? Why, the banks themselves! Either through the interest they charge their credit card customers (and, of course, the annual fee), the percentage they charge 'merchants' (shops, restaurants, hotels, etc.) or the processing costs they charge each other, American Express and Diners Card, the banks win every time.

The banks, however, no longer have it entirely their own way. In November 1986 a revolutionary new service was launched in the United Kingdom which provides a guarantee to merchants that cheques exceeding the drawer's limit will be honoured. This service, which is now called 'Transax', is now provided to 90 000 retail outlets in the UK, Ireland, France, Australia and New Zealand, including many of the major British high street names like Next, Saxone, Austin Reed and Halfords. The service guarantees personal cheques and business cheques up to a pre-arranged store limit, and all cheques are authorized using a free telephone call. If any guaranteed cheque subsequently bounces, Transax reimburses its full value to the merchant and then takes steps to recover the amount outstanding. The Transax service is therefore of considerable benefit to customers and merchants alike. Customers gain a further, potentially less expensive, means to purchase higher cost items and merchants gain a further means to stimulate sales which carries no risk and undue expense.

During the financial year 1994/95 Transax guaranteed some 9.5 million cheques with a combined value in excess of £1.5 billion, a significant increase over the previous year. Thus growth has been achieved despite a period of uncertain economic recovery and 'flat' high street spending, and underlines the concern that merchants feel concerning security of payment.

Transax is now the largest cheque guarantee company in the world outside the USA; the 'Transax' name is extremely well known and respected among a very wide range of outlets and the 'Transax' trademark is the registered property of Transax Financial Services Limited and, as such, inviolable. The strength of the legal title the company enjoys in its brand name and the investment it has made in developing its service means that the 'Transax' name now has considerable value in its own right. However, this is very far from the situation that applied back in June 1986.

Cheque Point/Chequepoint

When the founders of the business set up their cheque guarantee service in November 1986 they decided to call it Cheque Point Guarantee Limited. The name had a neat, logical ring to it, it described fully the key benefit of the service and even in its abbreviated form – 'Cheque Point' – lost none of its impact and relevance. The name had been suggested by the advertising agency they had hired to help them launch the new service and the agency had dutifully checked the name in Companies House to ensure that it was clear to use.

Imagine their horror, therefore, when, shortly after they had launched Cheque Point Guarantee Limited at a press reception in London, the directors received a letter from solicitors representing Chequepoint Bureau de Change claiming prior rights in the 'Chequepoint' name and threatening action for 'passing off' if they did not desist in its use. Not being Londoners, the directors of Cheque Point Guarantee Limited were unaware of Chequepoint's chain of bureaux de change which are largely confined to the West End. Nor was it easy to find out who owned Chequepoint Bureau de Change and how big it was (one of the first things you do when litigation is threatened!).

It is worth pausing here to remind ourselves what is meant by 'passing off'.

Passing Off

The common law tort of passing off is the original form of action for trademark owners to defend their rights and interests.

In its crudest definition, passing off is to ensure that 'nobody has any right to represent his goods (or services) as the goods (or services) of somebody else' (Lord Chief Justice Halsbury, 1896). This is, however, a rather simplistic view, and the outcome of passing off actions can be difficult to predict, as, although there is a line of precedence established over many years, essentially each case turns on its own facts and evidence.

Lord Diplock, however, in what has become known as the *Advocaat* case in 1979, ruled that in order to sustain an action for passing off the plaintiff must prove:

1. that there is misrepresentation;
2. made by a trader in the course of trade;
3. to prospective customers of his, or ultimate customers of goods or services supplied to him;
4. which is calculated to injure the business or goodwill of another trader (in the sense that this is a reasonably foreseeable consequence);
5. which causes actual damage to the business or goodwill of a trader by whom the action is brought.

The rights which passing off is designed to protect are only acquired through use in the UK, and as a general rule the greater the reputation, the greater the rights to protect. Thus Chequepoint Bureau de Change would need to prove that damage to its well-known business was caused by confusion arising from Cheque Point Guarantee's use of the name: a tall order perhaps in view of dissimilarity of the services provided by the two companies – Chequepoint Bureau de Change *only* provided foreign exchange services, and Cheque Point Guarantee *only* provided an indemnity service to merchants accepting sterling cheques.

Should the directors of Cheque Point Guarantee (now the defendants) oppose the action or should they give in and change their name? On the one hand they had just launched their business at considerable expense and were concerned lest they lose credibility (a vital ingredient in the service they supplied) with their hard-won customers; on the other, they were a tiny organization with limited resources confronting a mysterious opponent of unknown size and determination. They decided to fight.

The Hearing

The defendants thought it was important to convince the court that not only did their business offer a very different service from Chequepoint Bureau de Change – and therefore had no interest in competing with it – but that Chequepoint Bureau de Change's name had little recognition and goodwill and thus that there was little to 'pass off' as. In order to do the latter they commissioned MORI, the well-known market research company, to interview a sample of customers who had just used a Chequepoint Bureau de Change. MORI's interviewers asked the customers whether they could remember the name of the bureau de change they had just used and only a small minority could do so with any accuracy. Whether this was instrumental or not it is difficult to say, but on the second day of the hearing, having let slip that he still did not understand that you could cash a cheque at a bureau de change – thus questioning perhaps the relevance of the name in this connection – the judge called a recess. It was then that the defendants were approached by 'the other side' and offered a settlement if they agreed to change their name in six months, a clear sign that Chequepoint Bureau de Change was no longer confident that their case was cut and dried. As Cheque Point Guarantee was not in a position to fight a protracted action (a typical passing off action can take many months to complete, with high costs and no guarantee of a successful outcome), the owners agreed, with considerable reluctance, that they should relinquish the Cheque Point name.

Developing a New Name

With only six months to develop a new name and implement this in advertising sales literature, stationery, business forms, window stickers, and so on, there was no time for delay. Shortly after their court case, therefore, the directors of the business approached Interbrand, the international branding consultancy, with the brief that it should create and register a new name and identity for their business as rapidly as possible.

Interbrand's procedure for developing brandnames is entirely pragmatic. It is informed by the simple truth that, to be effective, brand names must help position the product or service they identify in an attractive and appealing way; they must be free of negative linguistic or cultural associations; and they must be available to use and protect as trademarks. Given the very large number of trademarks that already exist, it is therefore necessary to approach the creation of a new brand name in an open-minded and creative way. There is no point in following familiar, well-trodden creative 'routes' because it is almost certain that someone else has been there first. (Is there not a close similarity in meaning between the names 'Visa' and 'Access'?)

So the task of developing a name to replace 'Cheque Point' became not just a creative challenge but a strategic one: there were fundamental issues of identity and positioning at play and these needed to be addressed by Interbrand's project team in an appropriate, but original, fashion.

This, surprisingly, was easier than it seems. Looking back, the 'Cheque Point' name was a good one: it was certainly simple and appropriate. But it was neither particularly distinctive nor precise (as the court case showed!). It was felt, therefore, that a new name which alluded more closely to the nature of the service was required, and the creative team drew up a brief which specified a wide range of ideas ranging from the almost abstract 'Green Line' (signifying approval) to the very descriptive 'Cheque Mate' (reassuringly – if dangerously – close to the original name). Between these extremes lay a fertile middle ground where suggestion and innuendo could coexist comfortably with the exigencies of protectability.

It was from this middle ground that the 'Transax' name emerged, one of a list of 50 names selected for presentation to the client.

Fifty names may seem a great many – but a great deal of ore has to be fed into the hopper to produce a small amount of pure gold, the attractive and protectable brand name. It must be remembered too that the client had just come through a thoroughly disagreeable and damaging experience, so this time everything *had* to be right. And for Interbrand too the challenge was a stiff one. Whatever names it came up with would, inevitably, be compared with 'Cheque Point', which now had a significance to the client which quite outweighed its utility. Interbrand, therefore, had to ensure that the creative task was done thoroughly and that all possible 'avenues' were explored to provide the best possible choice.

At the presentation, therefore, names as varied as Assent (rejected because of the similarity to 'Access', but subsequently used by Barclays Bank!), Cheqtel (rejected because, while using 'check' or 'cheque' can produce attractive, relevant names, they were felt to be uncreative and somewhat redolent of the past) and Transax were submitted and discussed at considerable length. Transax was selected as a strong candidate and, together with several others, was then searched for availability as a service mark in Class 36 of the UK Trade Mark Register. In parallel, a small market research exercise was initiated, designed to establish the relative acceptability of the shortlisted names, taking into account the agreed criteria. This took place with approximately 100 potential users of the service and they came down overwhelmingly in favour of 'Transax'. The name meanwhile emerged unscathed from the legal searching process (which took only two weeks or so) and the clients decided to adopt the name – although it has to be said that they still retained a strong preference for Cheque Point!

Developing the Identity

Stage two of the exercise could now commence. This comprised two important exercises. First an application was filed to register 'Transax' in Class 36, thus insulating the name by staking prior rights, while solicitors formed Transax Financial Services Limited. Then Interbrand's design team started work on a visual identity for the new name, with the brief that this should be distinctively different from the old 'Cheque Point' logo – and of course from 'Access' and 'Visa' with whom it would compete for visibility at the point of sale.

Interbrand's designers developed a wide range of concepts.

Consider these designs in the context of the unique 'Transax' service. 'Transax' guarantees payment of the cheque and, in return, receives a small fee on each transaction. Many customers find the idea that their 'creditworthiness' is to be investigated by a third party before their cheque is accepted a little unnerving; retailers on the other hand want reassurance that 'Transax' is reliable and will stand behind its guarantee. The logo had, therefore, to help in two important respects: it had to reassure retailers and, at the same time, be approachable and not intimidating to consumers.

Not surprisingly, implementing the change of name had its difficulties. First, existing customers had to be reassured that the name change was being made for the very best of reasons, and would in no way affect the quality of the service they received. Next new stationery had to be ordered, brochures printed and window stickers redesigned (try persuading several thousand retailers to strip from their windows a heavily gummed decal and you will understand some of the pleasures of implementing a name change – Transax ended up offering £1 to charity for each 'Cheque Point' sticker returned!). However, the task was accomplished with relatively few problems, the Transax name was well received by old and new customers alike, by the ever-growing ranks of Transax employees, and eventually by the directors of the business!

■ Maintaining the 'Transax' Name

'When a man knows he is to be hanged in a fortnight', said Dr Johnson, 'it concentrates his mind wonderfully.' Had he experienced the horrors of a passing off action he no doubt would have expressed the same sentiment. Certainly the experience of the directors of Transax made them acutely aware of the need to protect their 'intellectual property' and this they have done with commendable zeal. Not only have they sought to protect through registration their interest in the 'Transax' name in the UK and internationally, but they have resisted successfully the attempts of more than one major British financial institution to register a similar name for its services!

■ Conclusions

What this case illustrates is the importance of careful trademark selection and registration. Unless you lay claim to and protect your trademark through the provisions the law allows, you will always be vulnerable to the depredations of third parties. Nowhere, arguably, is this more important than in the area of services, where the 'product' supplied is of an intangible nature, and the reputation of the supplier is all. As the name you use represents a 'proxy' for the quality of your services – and therefore your reputation – it is vital that you protect this. Unless these precautions are taken you can never be wholly confident that you alone will reap the benefits from the investment you have made in your business. In a sense the directors of Transax were fortunate that disaster befell them when it did – at a very early stage in the development of their business. They had the opportunity to start afresh with a new – and better! – identity, and have subsequently built one of the very few enduring new brands on the UK financial services scene.

CHAPTER 7

The Future of Trademarks and Branding

Future Trends

The major developments in trademarks and branding over the last 100 years have been the increased emphasis upon the intangible components of a brand's personality, the extension of the branding concept to services and not just products, and the increased protection at law afforded to brand owners. In addition, it has been increasingly recognized that a corporation can be every bit as much a 'brand' as a product or service while, at the same time, branding principles originally developed by major businesses in the USA and Europe have been adopted on a global basis.

All these trends are likely to continue for the foreseeable future and, in certain instances will strengthen. The increased interest over the last 30 years in service brands, for example, will certainly become stronger as whole areas of service products which are not branded at present and which are provided by myriads of local suppliers with widely varying standards of quality and service (for example, window cleaning) receive the 'branding treatment', possibly through franchise arrangements.

In the area of law, it is also certain that legal systems will afford increasingly strong protection to owners of intellectual property. Countries such as Japan, the USA and those of Western Europe fully recognize that their future prosperity depends not upon unique access to manufacturing skills or sources of raw material but upon their intellectual property assets. The USA has used the GATT (General Agreement on Tariffs and Trade) round of negotiations to link trading agreements with the extent to which countries control counterfeiting and enforce intellectual property rights. The World Intellectual Property Organization (WIPO), part of the United Nations, is also active in strengthening intellectual property laws around the world and ensuring that they are enforced; and the European Union is currently implementing a new trademark system to embrace the whole of the EU.

There are, however, in addition to these powerful trends, other developments which are likely to have a significant impact upon branding in the foreseeable future.

Brand Evaluation

Once the brand is recognized as a separable asset to which its owner has specific legal title and which is capable of producing cash flows in its own right, it becomes possible to treat the brand in many of the same ways as one treats any other form of valuable asset. Thus it can be bought, sold, licensed, even mortgaged. Central, however, to all these activities is brand valuation, and recent brand valuation activity has already led to companies considering their brands in a totally new light. Several companies, for example, have instructed corporate finance advisers to dispose of unwanted brands for the best possible price in much the same way as they would previously have instructed them to dispose of a subsidiary. Other companies such as Unilever (in the case of Cheseborough Ponds) and Ford (in the case of Jaguar), recognizing a gap in their brand portfolios, have repaired these deficiencies through acquisition.

Corporate raiders too, now recognize the value of brands and the fact that they are transferable and command high prices in the marketplace. KKR's acquisition of RJR Nabisco and, more recently, Grand Metropolitan's merger with Guinness were both based, in substantial measure, on a fundamental reappraisal of underlying brand values.

The recognition of specific value in brands can also lead to other forms of corporate activity. Once brand value is recognized and once it is recognized, too, that owners have specific title to their brands in the form of trademark registrations, it becomes possible to mortgage or lease brands and thus to use them as a form of security. In the USA, brand-based leases can be arranged at favourable rates and major fund-raising by brand owners is now being secured specifically on brands.

The licensing and franchising of brands will also become more common as brand owners seek to exploit more widely the equity in these valuable assets. It also seems inevitable that these two activities will become more expensive as their greater popularity with potential licensees and franchisees will enable brand owners to increase royalty rates. And for reasons of brand control as well as for tax purposes, major companies are increasingly adopting policies of internal brand licensing to both domestic and overseas subsidiaries.

Brand Management

The brand management function in companies has traditionally been a training ground for high flyers whose main task has been that of maintaining a link between the company and its advertising and sales promotion agencies. The increased focus on, and interest in, brands is leading to a fundamental reappraisal of the role and status of brand management. Brand managers are being required to take a much more entrepreneurial view of their brands and are now increasingly held accountable for their profitability and for a proper return on brand assets, both tangible and intangible. Several major companies are already redefining the marketing function and overhauling the brand management system. Recently one major brand owner, when appointing a new director to the board, specifically recognized this by changing the title from Director of Marketing to Director of Brands.

If brands are to become strong and successful, they must be managed proactively and in a rigorous and disciplined manner. The tasks facing brand managers now include the following:

- Formulating relevant and appropriate brand strategies consistent with the company's mission.
- Identifying, protecting and monitoring the consistency of each brand's positioning, personality and point of difference.
- Developing an appealing and distinctive communications strategy for each brand which supports its positioning and personality.
- Monitoring the brand's financial performance, product quality and market share performance against that of the competition.
- Developing new brand-related initiatives and making recommendations on all issues affecting each brand's future development including:
  - brand extension programmes
  - new product launches
  - expansion into new markets or new market segments.
- Reviewing and assessing the implications of competitor activity.

Brand managers cannot carry out any of the above without a profound understanding of the brand or brands for which they have responsibility.

This redefinition of the role of brand management and the elevation of brand management's status has resulted in a need for new discipline and new tools to allow better brand management to take place. Foremost among these is brand accounting, a practice which is currently followed by only a handful of companies. As well as brand accounting, much better and more systematic brand planning will be required together with the formal tracking of all aspects of brand performance and not just market share.

The Chairman of Verkade, one of Holland's major manufacturers of chocolate and biscuit products recently remarked that only a few years ago he saw himself as being primarily concerned with the financial strategy of the business. He has since totally redefined his role and now sees his primary responsibility as being the management and husbandry of the Verkade brand. The reappraisal of brand values and the specific attention which is being given to brands will inevitably mean that this process will be matched in other companies. These will adopt an increasingly brand-centric approach to their activities.

Table 7.1 The World's Best-Managed Brands in 1996 (not always the biggest, but the best performers)

Brand	Brand Value (%m.)	Premium to category* (%)	Category
1. Microsoft	11740	237	High tech
2. Louis Vuitton	4484	234	Cosmetics and fashion
3. Coca-Cola	39050	181	Soft drinks and juices
4. Gillette	9672	156	Men's toiletries
5. Playtex	670	118	Foundation garments
6. Braun	1321	106	Equipment
7. Levi's	6922	101	Apparel and accessories
8. Johnnie Walker Black Label	2790	99	Spirits
9. Jell-O	1525	96	Prepared food
10. GE	7420	95	Equipment
11. WD4O	233	94	Supplies
12. Monopoly	145	92	Toys and games
13. Marlboro	38714	91	Tobacco
14. Tampax	1464	91	Personal care
15. Kellogg's	11003	89	Prepared food
16. Guinness	2318	85	Beers
17. Chivas Regal	2296	84	Spirits
18. Dr Pepper	1133	81	Soft drinks and juices
19. Courvoisier	935	76	Spirits
20. Goodyear	4660	72	Tyres

* The difference between the brand's value to its current owner and what a typical company in the same category would achieve.
© Financial Week/Interbrand.

Brand Extension versus New Brand Development

It has recently been suggested by several commentators, particularly in the USA, that the days of new brand development are over and that no company would ever again be so foolhardy as to attempt it. While it seems clear that, given a choice between new brand development and brand extension, brand owners should give serious consideration to the extension route, none the less in very many instances the option of extending simply does not exist. Although a company may prefer to extend its brands or to acquire existing ones, if these routes are not available, then it may have no choice but to develop a new brand. However, a number of strategies can be used to reduce the risk of new brand development, such as the exploration of other markets for new brand ideas and more meaningful market research.

Internationalization

Major international brand owners have, during the 1980s and early 1990s, substantially increased their hold on world markets, both through the winning of larger market shares and through the acquisition of other branded goods businesses. In the EU, for example, major brand owners have looked anxiously at establishing a powerful brand position across Europe. This is because they have recognized that one of the implications of a larger trading group and of better communications will be the increased dominance of the more powerful international brands. This process is likely to continue for the foreseeable future, though new niche brands, often those which were originally based on local tastes and habits, will constantly be introduced and will provide consumers with continuing variety and interest.

Private Label Brands

Manufacturers have become increasingly concerned in recent years about the growth of retailer private label and in Britain it is now estimated that some 37 per cent of all grocery expenditure is made on retailers' – rather than manufacturers' – brands. The trend is Europe-wide and reflects generally the degree of retailer concentration that is present. The efficient Swiss lead the way with the mighty Migros chain, one of the most dominant forces in European private label; but at the other end of the scale, in countries such as Ireland and Portugal, where retailer concentration is relatively low, private label is weak.

While it seems that, in Britain, the penetration of private label will probably 'peak' at around 40 per cent, this is still an immense market and represents a formidable loss of share for the manufacturers brands. There is however little prospect of private label brands destroying those of the major manufacturers, if only because many smaller retailers are unable to follow the private label route. None the less there seems no reason why manufacturers' brands should have a divine right to the majority of any market.

Private label brands have gained share because they are innovative, attractive, well packaged, well priced and frequently offer the consumer satisfactions which manufacturers' brands do not. Manufacturers need to respond to this phenomenon in a much more constructive way than they have done to date. They need to be more innovative, they need to reduce the costs of new product development and launch and they also need considerably to reduce the timescale required to bring new products to market.

Furthermore, the phenomenon of private label seems likely to become much more powerfully established in markets such as the United States, as integrated national retail chains develop at the expense of local or regional operators.

■ The 'Lookalike' Phenomenon

One of the most vexed marketing issues to have surfaced in recent years in developed markets is that of retailer 'lookalike' brands. Such lookalikes have been particularly evident in Britain but the problem is one which confronts brand owners in other countries too, particularly in the USA, Canada and Australasia.

Lookalikes are retailer private label brands which mimic the trade dress of the brand leader. Recent British examples include Classic Cola from J. Sainsbury, a brand whose overall get-up is clearly based upon Coca-Cola; Tesco's Anti-Dandruff Shampoo, a product which bears an uncanny resemblance to Procter & Gamble's Head & Shoulders Frequent brand; and Tesco's Unbelievable vegetable fat spread, a clear copy of I Can't Believe It's Not Butter from Van den Bergh Foods, part of Unilever.

The lookalikes try to avoid direct trademark infringement by choosing names which do not infringe those of the brand leader (though, in the case of Tesco's Unbelievable, the punning reference to the original brand is clear) and, therefore, the brand leader normally has no legal recourse based upon registered trademark rights. The only other potential recourse, under current English law, is 'passing-off', but such actions are notoriously difficult and expensive and, in practice, the irate brand owner usually has little option but to bite the bullet or to appeal to the retailer's sense of fair play.

The problem is, of course, exacerbated by the fact that retailers are both competitors and customers of the brand owners who are particularly reluctant to adopt a massively confrontational stance *vis-à-vis* such important customers. And conversely, the retailers themselves are coming under such price competition that strategies, such as lookalikes, which might have been unacceptable to them some years ago are now seen to be justified on commercial grounds.

The irony of the retailer lookalike brands (or 'copycat' brands as they are sometimes called) is that they are not directed at weak or under-supported brands but at brands which have been well and consistently managed and supported by their owners. Indeed, the purpose of the lookalikes is, clearly, to compete by unfair means with brands where conventional, fair private label tactics have failed.

Sainsbury's Classic Cola is an example. For many years Sainsbury's, a huge British grocery retailer with a turnover of some $20 billion, has had a private label cola but, even at a somewhat cheaper price, it made only modest headway against Coca-Cola and Pepsi-Cola. Then in April 1994 Sainsbury launched its lookalike and Coca-Cola fell from around 70 per cent of Sainsbury's cola sales to around 20 per cent, while 'private label' (the new lookalike) rose from around 20 per cent to near 70 per cent, a share which it has maintained.

Sainsbury's attribute the success of Classic Cola to its superior taste (though in fact their previous private label cola was of high quality) and justify their copying of the Coca-Cola trade dress on the grounds of providing value to consumers and the fact that they are merely supplying the 'visual cues' of the sector. They also maintain that as manufacturers copy each others' trade dress, why should not they be able to do the same?

In fact, the lookalike brands are not priced at a huge discount to manufacturers' brands. Rather, they are priced quite close to the manufacturer's brand and at a substantial premium to conventional own-label. Clearly, they are an attempt by retailers to buy products at private label prices and sell them at close to manufacturers' brand prices without any of the costs of brand development or brand support.

Unfortunately, and unlike many other countries, Britain does not yet have Unfair Competition or (as it is known in Australia) Trade Practices legislation. It is high time that Britain introduced new legislation as it is certain that the retailer lookalikes have crossed the boundary between what is fair in business and what is not fair. And if lookalikes are allowed to continue we shall not only see the destruction of leading brands but a massive reduction in brand-related economic activity and investment.

■ The Role of the Corporate Brand

The corporation is, in effect a brand – it needs to present itself in a controlled, appropriate and differentiated fashion so as to assume in the minds of its various audiences a coherent and appropriate brand personality. Naturally, corporations seek to communicate with their audiences in a variety of ways and, like human personalities, they present themselves in somewhat different ways to different audiences even though the overall personality profile should be integrated, appropriate and appealing. In all companies a properly constructed, thorough, well-implemented corporate identity system helps position the company and its products, assists in communication and motivation, imparts messages to both suppliers and investors and focuses the power of the media. Furthermore, it ensures the proper participation of subsidiaries, divisions and operating companies and ensures that the overall aims and direction of the company are well understood. In our experience corporate identity and corporate presentation is becoming an increasingly important factor in international success.

■ Branding Industrial Products

It is sometimes assumed that branding is a phenomenon confined to consumer products; that brand loyalty is a form of habitual, non-rational behaviour which applies to (mainly) soap flakes and detergents but which has no chance of survival in the more 'rational' world of 'serious' products such as electric motors, office machinery or therapeutic drugs. However, some of the strongest brands exist in non-consumer products sectors – examples include Hibitane, an antiseptic surgical scrub from Zeneca, Salamander, a thermal ceramic for use in crucibles, Laserjet, a laser printer from Hewlett-Packard, and RoundUp, a herbicide from Monsanto. The reason for the strength of such brands is that brands serve exactly the same function in industrial markets as in consumer markets – they provide the consumer with a guarantee of quality, origin, value and performance; they provide a form of convenient short-hand for decision-making and they help to simplify complexity. For the brand owner they provide a means of talking directly to the consumer; thus they serve as a focus for consumer loyalty and as a means of 'capturing' promotional investment. They thus become strong and enduring assets which increase in strength and value with use and help the manufacturer resist competitive attack. Branding is certain to become an increasingly important factor in industrial markets in the future although it is clear that in many industrial companies the brand management function, as it is understood and applied in the area of fast-moving consumer goods, is either non-existent or in its infancy. A significant trend, therefore, will be towards the active management of the intangible attributes of industrial brands and, therefore, the increased use of specialist advertising agencies and sales promotion companies.

■ Branding Pharmaceutical Products

Throughout the USA and Europe there is heavy and increasing pressure by government and health insurance providers to reduce the price of drugs and to encourage self-medication. This inexorable process, which is bound to be taken up elsewhere, is forcing the world pharmaceutical industry fundamentally to re-appraise its activities and profound structural changes are underway as a result. It is forecast that, with rationalization, the industry will segment between a hard core of 15–20 truly global manufacturers who will continue to invest heavily in research and development; a large number of medium-sized companies operating at a regional or local level who will be active in the supply of, mainly, generic (non-proprietary) drugs, and a small number of 'hot shot' research-based specialists, located mainly in the USA and Europe and engaged mainly in the development of new drugs. What is also forecast is the increasing use of branding to help the major manufacturers exploit fully the potential of their products both during and after the lifetime of their patents. A strong brand name – which in effect 'speaks for' the reputation of the product – can not only help stave off a rapid decline in sales in the immediate post-patent period but can provide valuable 'springboard' to the rapidly growing market for over-the-counter medicines. Companies like Glaxo Wellcome, with Zantac and Zovirax, understand that strategic value of their brands and have successfully introduced OTC versions of these breakthrough drugs.

Ten Rules of Good Brand Management

Brand management is a difficult and complex process – and unlikely in the future, due to the great importance of brands to corporate welfare and the scrutiny this will attract, to get any easier. Although it is difficult to prescribe a set number of rules and guidelines for brand management, the following ten general rules should, wherever possible, in the future, be observed.

1. Cherish your Brands

Brands are valuable and important assets and must be cared for by everyone in the organization. It is vital to ensure that brands have a central role within the organization.

2. Account for your Brands

Ensure that management reporting and accounting systems are constructed on a brand-by-brand basis. Know your true brand profitability.

3. Manage Brands Conservatively

Do not change a brand's positioning and personality unless there is a very good reason to do so. Listen to consumers and act on their feed back. Build for the long term, do not exploit for short-term gain.

4. Take Brand Management Seriously

Treat brand management as a serious function within the organization and give authority to those responsible. Remember that everyone shares in the brand management function – the chairman and the chief executive are just as relevant to the brand management function as junior brand managers.

5. Maintain Responsibility for Brands

Your brands are your responsibility. Do not surrender responsibility for brands to an advertising agency, overseas distributor, joint venture partner, or external licensee. Ultimate strategic decision-making responsibility should always rest with the brand owner.

6. Maintain a Point of Difference

Consumers have many brands from which to choose and most of these have similar functional values of quality, efficacy and reliability. A company must always strive to create and maintain a point of uniqueness, preferably both functionally and emotionally. What differentiates brands are emotional values that underline the brand's personality. These are often to a greater or lesser extent based on a functional point of difference. Ensure that your brands have genuine and sustainable points of difference.

■ 7. Exploit the Equity in your Brands

Exploit the equity of existing brands by extending their use into new product areas. But be careful – avoid any initiatives that may dilute the brand. Whenever you are carrying out a brand extension programme, always ensure that the brand's core values are not diluted in any way.

■ 8. Review your Brand Portfolio

Brands are separable, transferable assets. Dispose of brands that have no strategic purpose or potential and consider replacing them with brands that do. Remember that it is only those brands with strong differentiation and market leadership potential that will survive for the long term.

■ 9. Consider the International Arena

Global branding is here to stay. International brands are more powerful, more profitable and more valuable than national brands. If you do not think internationally, you run the risk of being over-run by more aggressive internationally-orientated competitors.

■ 10. Protect your Brands

Trademark registration affords powerful rights at low cost. Ensure you have clear title to your brands in all countries, and in all categories of goods and services likely to be of interest. Police trademarks with great vigilance.

APPENDIX I

Trademark Classification

Goods

□ *Class 1*

Chemicals used in industry, science and photography, as well as in agriculture, horticulture and forestry; unprocessed artificial resins, unprocessed plastics; manures; fire extinguishing compositions; tempering and soldering preparations; chemical substances for preserving foodstuffs; tanning substances; adhesives used in industry.

□ *Class 2*

Paints, varnishes, lacquers; preservatives against rust and against deterioration of wood; colorants; mordants; raw natural resins; metals in foil and powder form for painters, decorators, printers and arts.

□ *Class 3*

Bleaching preparations and other substances for laundry use; cleaning, polishing, scouring and abrasive preparations; soaps; perfumery, essential oils, cosmetics, hair lotions; dentifrices.

□ *Class 4*

Industrial oils and greases; lubricants; dust absorbing, wetting and binding compositions; fuels (including motor spirit) and illuminates; candles, wicks.

□ *Class 5*

Pharmaceutical, veterinary and sanitary preparations; dietetic substances adapted for medical use, food for babies; plasters, materials for dressings; material for stopping teeth, dental wax; disinfectants; preparations for destroying vermin; fungicides, herbicides.

□ *Class 6*

Common metals and their alloys; metal building materials; transportable buildings of metal; materials of metal for railway tracks; non-electric cables and wires of common metal; ironmongery, small items of metal hardware; pipes and tubes of metal; safes; goods of common metal not included in other classes; ores.

□ *Class 7*

Machines and machine tools; motors (except for land vehicles); machine coupling and belting (except for land vehicles); agricultural implements; incubators for eggs.

□ *Class 8*

Hand tools and implements (hand-operated); cutlery, forks and spoons; side arms; razors.

□ *Class 9*

Scientific, nautical, surveying, electric, photographic, cinematographic, optical, weighing, measuring, signalling, checking (supervision), life-saving and teaching apparatus and instruments; apparatus for recording, transmission or reproduction of sound or images; magnetic data carriers, recording discs; automatic vending machines and mechanisms for coin-operated apparatus; cash registers, calculating machines and data processing equipment; fire-extinguishing apparatus.

□ *Class 10*

Surgical, medical, dental and veterinary apparatus and instruments, artificial limbs, eyes and teeth; orthopaedic articles; suture materials.

□ *Class 11*

Apparatus for lighting, heating, steam generating, cooking, refrigerating, drying, ventilating, water supply and sanitary purposes.

□ *Class 12*

Vehicles; apparatus for locomotion by land, air or water.

☐ *Class 13*

Firearms; ammunition and projectiles; explosives; fireworks.

☐ *Class 14*

Precious metals and their alloys and goods in precious metals or coated therewith, not included in other classes; jewellery, precious stones; horological and chronometric instruments.

☐ *Class 15*

Musical instruments.

☐ *Class 16*

Paper, cardboard and goods made from these materials, not included in other classes; printed matter; bookbinding material; photographs; stationery; adhesives for stationery or household purposes; artists' materials; paint brushes; typewriters and office requisites (except furniture); instructional and teaching material (except apparatus); plastic materials for packaging (not included in other classes); playing cards; printers' type; printing blocks.

☐ *Class 17*

Rubber, gutta-percha, gum, asbestos, mica and goods made from these materials and not included in other classes; plastics in extruded form for use in manufacture; packing, stopping and insulating materials; flexible pipes, not of metal.

☐ *Class 18*

Leather and imitations of leather and goods made of these materials and not included in other classes; animal skins, hides; trunks and travelling bags; umbrellas, parasols and walking sticks; whips, harness and saddlery.

☐ *Class 19*

Building materials (non-metallic); non-metallic rigid pipes for building; asphalt, pitch and bitumen; non-metallic transportable buildings; monuments, not of metal.

□ *Class 20*

Furniture, mirrors, picture frames; goods (not included in other classes) of wood, cork, reed, cane, wicker, horn, bone, ivory, whalebone, shell, amber, mother-of-pearl, meerschaum and substitutes for all these materials, or of plastics.

□ *Class 21*

Household or kitchen utensils and containers (not of precious metal or coated therewith); combs and sponges; brushes (except paint brushes); brush-making materials; articles for cleaning purposes; steelwool; unworked or semi-worked glass (except glass used in building); glassware, porcelain and earthenware not included in other classes.

□ *Class 22*

Ropes, string, nets, tents, awnings, tarpaulins, sails, sacks and bags (not included in other classes); padding and stuffing materials (except of rubber or plastics); raw fibrous textile materials.

□ *Class 23*

Yarns and threads, for textile use.

□ *Class 24*

Textiles and textile goods, not included in other classes; bed and table covers.

□ *Class 25*

Clothing, footwear, headgear.

□ *Class 26*

Lace and embroidery, ribbons and braid; buttons, hooks and eyes, pins and needles; artificial flowers.

□ *Class 27*

Carpets, rugs, mats and matting, linoleum and other materials for covering existing floors; wall hangings (non-textile).

□ *Class 28*

Games and playthings; gymnastic and sporting articles not included in other classes; decorations for Christmas trees.

□ *Class 29*

Meat, fish, poultry and game; meat extracts; preserved, dried and cooked fruits and vegetables; jellies, jams; eggs, milk and milk products; edible oils and fats; salad dressings; preserves.

□ *Class 30*

Coffee, tea, cocoa, sugar, rice, tapioca, sago, artificial coffee; flour and preparations made from cereals, bread, pastry and confectionery, ices; honey, treacle; yeast, baking-powder; salt, mustard; vinegar, sauces (except salad dressings); spices; ice.

□ *Class 31*

Agricultural horticultural and forestry products and grains not included in other classes; living animals; fresh fruits and vegetables; seeds, natural plants and flowers; foodstuffs for animals, malt.

□ *Class 32*

Beers; mineral and aerated waters and other non-alcoholic drinks; fruit drinks and fruit juices; syrups and other preparations for making beverages.

□ *Class 33*

Alcoholic beverages (except beers).

□ *Class 34*

Tobacco; smokers' articles; matches.

■ Services

□ *Class 35*

Advertising and business.

☐ *Class 36*

Insurance and financial.

☐ *Class 37*

Construction and repair.

☐ *Class 38*

Communication.

☐ *Class 39*

Transportation and storage.

☐ *Class 40*

Material treatment.

☐ *Class 41*

Education and entertainment.

☐ *Class 42*

Miscellaneous.

APPENDIX II

Trademark Application Form

TRADEMARK/SERVICE MARK APPLICATION, PRINCIPAL REGISTER, WITH DECLARATION	MARK (Word(s) and/or Design)	CLASS NO. (If known)

TO THE ASSISTANT SECRETARY AND COMMISSIONER OF PATENTS AND TRADEMARKS:

APPLICANT'S NAME:

APPLICANT'S BUSINESS ADDRESS: ____________________
(Display address exactly as ____________________
it should appear on registration) ____________________
____

APPLICANT'S ENTITY TYPE: (Check one and supply requested information)

	Individual - Citizen of (Country):
	Partnership - State where organized (Country, if appropriate): ____________________ Names and Citizenship (Country) of General Partners: ____________________ ____________________ ____________________
	Corporation - State (Country, if appropriate) of Incorporation:
	Other (Specify Nature of Entity and Domicile):

GOODS AND/OR SERVICES

Applicant requests registration of the trademark/service mark shown in the accompanying drawing in the United States Patent and Trademark Office on the Principal Register established by the Act of July 5, 1946 (15 U.S.C. 1051 et. seq., as amended) for the following goods/services (SPECIFIC GOODS AND/OR SERVICES MUST BE INSERTED HERE): ____________________
____
____
____
____
____

BASIS FOR APPLICATION: (Check boxes which apply, but never both the first AND second boxes, and supply requested information related to each box checked.)

[ ] Applicant is using the mark in commerce on or in connection with the above identified goods/services. (15 U.S.C. 1051(a), as amended.) Three specimens showing the mark as used in commerce are submitted with this application.

- Date of first use of the mark in commerce which the U.S. Congress may regulate (for example, interstate or between the U.S. and a foreign country): ____________
- Specify the type of commerce: ____________
  (for example, interstate of between the U.S. and a specified foreign country)
- Date of first use anywhere (the same as or before use in commerce date): ____________
- Specify manner or mode of use of mark on or in connection with the goods/services: ____________

____

(for example, trademark is applied to labels, service mark is used in advertisements)

[ ] Applicant has a bona fide intention to use the mark in commerce on or in connection with the above identified goods/services. (15 U.S.C. 1051(b), as amended.)

- Specify intended manner or mode of use of mark on or in connection with the goods/services:

(for example, trademark will be applied to labels, service mark will be used in advertisements)

[ ] Applicant has a bona fide intention to use the mark in commerce on or in connection with the above identified goods/services, and asserts a claim of priority based upon a foreign application in accordance with 15 U.S.C. 1126(d), as amended.

- Country of foreign filing: ____________
- Date of foreign filing: ____________

[ ] Applicant has a bona fide intention to use the mark on or in connection with the above identified goods/services and, accompanying this application, submits a certification or certified copy of a foreign registration in accordance with 15 U.S.C. 1126(e), as amended.

- Country of registration: ____________
- Registration number: ____________

NOTE: Declaration, on Reverse Side, MUST be Signed

PTO Form 1478 (REV. 5/91)
OMB No. 06510009 (Exp. 6/92)

U.S. DEPARTMENT OF COMMERCE/Patent and Trademark Office

DECLARATION

The undersigned being hereby warned that willful false statements and the like so made are punishable by fine or imprisonment, or both, under 18 U.S.C. 1001, and that such willful false statements may jeopardize the validity of the application or any resulting registration, declares that he/she is properly authorized to execute this application on behalf of the applicant; he/she believes the applicant to be the owner of the trademark/service mark sought to be registered, or, if the application is being filed under 15 U.S.C. 1051(b), he/she believes applicant to be entitled to use such mark in commerce; to the best of his/her knowledge and belief, no other person, firm, corporation, or association has the right to use the above identified mark in commerce, either in the identical form thereof or in such near resemblance thereto as to be likely, when used on or in connection with the goods/services of such other person, to cause confusion, or to cause mistake, or to deceive; and that all statements made of his/her own knowledge are true and that all statements made on information and belief are believed to be true.

____________________ ____________________

DATE SIGNATURE

____________________ ____________________

TELEPHONE NUMBER PRINT OR TYPE NAME AND POSITION

INSTRUCTIONS AND INFORMATION FOR APPLICANT

TO RECEIVE A FILING DATE, THE APPLICATION MUST BE COMPLETED AND SIGNED BY THE APPLICANT AND SUBMITTED ALONG WITH:

1. The prescribed FEE ($200.00) for each class of goods/services listed in the application;
2. A DRAWING PAGE displaying the mark in conformance with 37 CFR 2.52;

3. If the application is based on the use of the mark in commerce, THREE (3) SPECIMENS (evidence) of the mark as used in commerce for each class of goods/services listed in the application. All three specimens may be in the nature of: (a) labels showing the mark which are placed on the goods; (b) photographs of the mark as it appears on the goods, (c) brochures or advertisements showing the mark as used in connection with the services.
4. An APPLICATION WITH DECLARATION (this form) - The application must be signed in order for the application to receive a filing date. Only the following person may sign the declaration, depending on the applicant's legal entity: (a) the individual applicant; (b) an officer of the corporate applicant; (c) one general partner of a partnership applicant; (d) all joint applicants.

SEND APPLICATION FORM, DRAWING PAGE, FEE, AND SPECIMENS (IF APPROPRIATE) TO:

U.S. DEPARTMENT OF COMMERCE
Patent and Trademark Office, Box TRADEMARK
Washington, D.C. 20231

Additional information concerning the requirements for filing an application is available in a booklet entitled Basic Facts About Trademarks, which may be obtained by writing to the above address or by calling: (703) 305-HELP.

This form is estimated to take 15 minutes to complete. Time will vary depending upon the needs of the individual case. Any comments on the amount of time you require to complete this form should be sent to the Office of Management and Organization, U.S. Patent and Trademark Office, U.S. Department of Commerce, Washington, D.C., 20231, and to the Office of Information and Regulatory Affairs, Office of Management and Budget, Washington, D.C. 20503.

Bibliography

Interbrand, *Brands: An International Review by Interbrand* (Mercury Books, 1989)
McGrath, K. and S. Elias with S. Shena, *Trademarks: How to Name a Business and Product* (published in USA: Nolo Press, 1992)
Michaels, A., *A Practical Guide to Trade Marks* (ESC Publishing, 1982)
Murphy, J. *Branding – A Key Marketing Tool* (London: Macmillan, 1987)
——— (ed.) *Brand Valuation*, 2nd edn (Business Books, 1989)
———, *Brand Strategy* (Director Books, 1990)
——— and M. Rowe, *How to Design Trademarks and Logos* (Graphic Library, 1988)
Pearson, H. and C. Miller, *Commercial Exploitation of Intellectual Property* (Blackstone Press, 1990)
Stobart, P. (ed.) *Brand Power* (London: Macmillan, 1994)

Index